ENCYCLOPAEDIA OF CRIMINOLOGY

ENCYCLOPAEDIA OF CRIMINOLOGY

Compiled & Edited by

SURENDRA P. SINGH

RELIANCE PUBLISHING HOUSE
NEW DELHI (INDIA)

First Published 2002

Price: Rs. [redacted].)

Price charged is inclusive of delivery

ISBN : 81-7510-140-7 (H.B.)

Published by
Dr. S.K. Bhatia (Life Member ILA & INSA)
for **RELIANCE PUBLISHING HOUSE**
3026/7H, Ranjit Nagar,
New Delhi-110 008 Ph. 5737377/5852605

Composed by
Elegant Printographics
74, Savera Apartments,
Sector-13, Plot-5, Rohini,
Delhi-110085 Ph. : 7567413

Printed by : **S. S. S. Printers**
New Delhi.

Many commit the same crimes with a very different result. One bears a cross for his crime; another a crown

— JUVENAL : Satires

PREFACE

The crime and criminals are as old as the human civilization and with the surge in crime the laws were formed and enacted by various rulers of the land. Any act punishable by law is a crime, and its scientific study criminology. The science of/or which is used in the court of law is forensic science, then there is forensic medicine i.e. application of medical knowledge of legal problems or situations. Although criminology and forensic science or methods have been in use down the ages in history, but its scientific status is of recent origin.

Although not everyone agrees on the meaning of crime and criminals, there is considerable controversy in criminology. Some authorities have suggested that the proper subject matter encompasses only those persons convicted in a criminal court of criminal violations of law. Other criminologists include within the populations of criminal persons who have been arrested but not convicted. But majority of people associated with criminality focus on individuals who have violated criminal laws.

The references about medical testimony and punishment can be found in Vedas and Manusmriti. The Vedas prohibited abortion, Manu forbade the execution of pregnant women and enjoined the statements of insane, of the drunk and children. The code of Hammurabi, ruler of Babylon (2000 BC) was the first feather in the cap of the history of legal medicine. The code regulated medical practice and laid down punishment for physicians who failed in their duties, similar codes have also been confirmed to have existed in ancient China, India, Persia, Rome, Egypt etc. the 'Constituto Criminalis Carolina (1532) by Charles- V, the Roman emperor can be regarded as the dawn of legal medicine.

The social character in conceptions of crime is evident in the fact that the number of acts regarded as crimes have steadily risen over the past several hundred years and law making bodies have created more and more criminal statutes. Definition and explanations of criminal acts are subject to variations from place to place. The constitution of law or process of law making reflect social behaviour. Particular criminal laws have identifiable antecedents; reasons exists for the emergence of laws at some particular time or in some specific place.

This encyclopaedia is a unique, comprehensive and up-to-date compilation of terms from criminology, the entries also elucidate the unique slang used in police work, law, drug and prison culture across the English speaking world. The additions from forensic science, psychology, sociology, medicine, toxicology, social medicine and biochemistry make the collection more authentic and complete.

SURENDRA P. SINGH

A

Abactor:

A cattle or horse rustler who steals entire herds.

Abandonment:

The willful, intentional relinquishing of one's property or claim to it, without naming a new owner.

The giving up of an intention to commit a crime. The general view is that it may not be use as a defense in court as long as there is a clear and unequivocal intent upon the part of the accused to carry out the crime at one time.

Leaving behind one's matrimonial, parental, or custodial responsibilities.

Abasia:

The inability to walk due to the effect of drugs or alcohol.

Abbott:

A tablet of nembutal.

Abduct:

The forced removal or carrying away of a person. The unlawful removal of a wife, child or ward by any means. The unlawful removal of a woman for purposes of prostitution, slavery, or rape.

Abductor:

A persons who forcibly removes or carries a person away against that person's will

Abet:

To aid in or encourage the commission of a crime

Abetment:

The act of persuading or helping in the commission of a crime.

Abettor:

One who instigates, encourages or aids in the commission of a crime.

Abiding conviction:

A clear conviction of guilt arrived at by a careful examination of evidence. This a term frequently used by judges during their instruction to the jury.

Abjure:

To foreswear one's rights. Privileges or position under oath.

Abnormal criminal:

A psychopath or psychotic person who has a tendency toward crime.

Abnormal sex:

Any criminal sexual behavior except adultery or fornication.

Abolitionism:

The movement to abolish slavery or, in modern times, prisons.

Abort:

To terminate an action before it is complete. To terminate a pregnancy prematurely.

Aborticide:

Termination of a pregnancy while the fetus is still in the uterus.

Abortifacient:

A substance capable of producing an abortion, usually taken orally.

Abortion:

The termination of an unborn child's life while it is in the womb; the forced or spontaneous expulsion of a fetus from the womb.

Abraham's hempen elixir:

Death by hanging, named after the hemp tree Abrahams balm.

Abreaction:

The process of discharge or release of emotional tension associated with a repressed conflict, memory or idea; often accompanied by recall of a painful experience.

Abscess:

A local infection of tissues, commonly found on drug addicts who use unsterile needles.

Absolute liability:

Having responsibility without negligence or fault.

Absolve:

To free from guilt or responsibility.

Abstinence syndrome:

Symptoms accompanying with drawal or abstinence from alcohol or other (narcotic) drugs.

Abstinence:

The voluntary avoidance of alcohol or other drugs.

Abstraction:

The process, whereby thoughts or ideas are generalized and dissociated from particular concrete instance or material objects. Concreteness in proverb interpretation suggests an impairment in abstraction; seen in schizophrenia.

Abuse:

An overindulgence in or improper use of treatment of drugs, alcohol, sex or other pleasures. To mistreat a person, especially by a verbal or physical attack.

Excessive or improper use of substances, usually psychoactive, which may result in damage to health or increase risk of such damage.

Abusive dosage:

The amount of a substance necessary to achieve the euphoric state sought by the user.

Abusive language:

Harsh, derogatory language used during a verbal attack.

Acapulco gold:

Golden colored marijuana from south western Mexico.

Acapulco red:

Reddish marijuana grown in Acapulco,

Accelerant:

A highly combustible material used by arsonist to start or speed a fire.

Accelerants:

Flammable materials used by arsonists to accelerate the burning of property, or to increase the amount of destruction.

Accessory:

One who helps or provides assistance to a criminal or the commission of a crime, but is not the chief actor in the offense.

A person who aids or contributes before, during, or after an unlawful act in a subordinate or secondary capacity:

Accidental criminal:

One who commits criminals offense without intending to do so.

Accidental killing:

A death that result from an act performed lawfully, where no harm was thought to be possible.

Accidental:

An inmate who has been imprisoned for a social offense, or any prisoner who is not a true criminal in the eyes of this fellow prisoner.

Acco collar:

An arrest made solely to fulfill an officer's quota.

Accommodartion arrest:

A pre-arranged arrest performed by corrupt police officers to hoodwink the general public.

Accomplice liability:

Being held criminally responsible for one's participation be-

fore, during or after the commission of crime.

Accomplice:

One who willingly and knowingly takes part with another in the commission of a crime

Acquittal:

A setting free or deliverance from a charge by verdict.

Addess :

The madam of a whorehouse,

Addiction:

See dependence.

Adjudication:

A formal judicial decision that ends a proceeding by a judgment of conviction, acquittal, or dismissal.

Adjustment:

Functional, and often transitory alteration or accomodation by which one can adapt himself better to the immediate environment. In adjustment disorder, there occur maladaptive reactions to identifiable life events or circumstances.

Administrative segregation:

The confinement of prisoners to individual cells.

Admissible evidence:

Evidence deemed material and relevant so as to be allowed in a judicial proceeding.

Admissible:

That which is fitting and proper for consideration in court.

Admission:

An acknowledgement that a certain fact is true.

Admitting to bail:

Releasing a defendant upon his posting bail.

Adult book:

Any pornographic publication

Adult entertainment center:

Adult business district.

Adult fiction:

A pornographic novel.

Adulterine/Adulterous bastard:

A child born to parents who are not legally married or are both or one of them married to another person.

Adultery:

Sexual intercourse involving one who is married to another who is not that person's spouse. Some jurisdictions find this a crime only when the women in this triangle is married. Types of adultery include; single, where only one party is married; double or compound, where both adulterers are married; or open and notorious, where the adulterous couple openly live together.

Advocate:

Lawyer

Aeschorolalia:

A tirade of obscene language from a psychotic patient.

Affect, blunted:

Severe restriction in intensity of emotional or affective expression.

Affect, flat:

Absence or near absence of any signs of affective expression.

Affect, inappropriate or incongruous:

Disharmony between affect and the idea, thought or speech accompanying it. Or, the affect is not in keeping with the external circumstances.

Affect:

The subjective and immediate experience of emotion attached to ideas or mental representation of objects. Normally appropriate, and of adequate range and depth (intensity). May be happy, sad, irritable, angry, or anxious. Sudden and abrupt changes in affect, known as lability of affect are seen in mania and organic psychiatric disorders.

Affective insanity:

All forms of insanity which deal with the feeling or emotions and affect one's ethical and social relations.

Affidavit :

A written statement made under oath or an attachment to a warrant wherein the police detail probable cause.

Affidavit men:

Individuals who swore in court to anything in return for money

Affidavit:

A written statement made voluntarily and verified under oath before am authorized person.

Affinity scams:

Bunco frauds which target a specific ethnic or racial group to entice victims to invest in illegal investment schemes.

Affray:

Public showing of violence by at least two people that leads to a disturbance of others in the area.

African black:

Marijuana grown in Africa or colored black.

Age of consent:

The age at which someone is legally able to give informed consent to sex; one commits statutory rape if one has sex with another who has not reached the age prescribed in a jurisdiction.

Aggaravated assault:

An attack by one person on another with the purpose of inflicting servere bodily injury; usually involving a weapon or some other means likely to cause death or serious bodily harm.

Agitation:

Marked restlessness and excessive motor activity , accompanied by anxiety.

AIDS:

(acquired immunodeficiency syndrome)—A fatal disease which prevents the proper functioning of the body's immune system caused by the human immunodeficiency virus—HIV. People with AIDS are unable to resist or fight off opportunist diseases {e.g. pneumonia or cancer), serious viral and bacterial infections. HIV is spread by any activity which results in direct bloodstream contact with an infected partner's body fluid (e.g. blood or semen). It is also passed to infants during pregnancy or by breast- feeding. It is easily spread by the use of shared infected needles by drug abusers. Because of the large mucosal surface area within the vagina and the quantity of semen ejaculated during-intercourse AIDS spreads much more easily to women from men. Although small quantities of HIV are found in tears and saliva, no cases of its spread via either of these are recorded. AIDS is not spread by usual social contact such as hugging or shaking hands, through breathing near infected people or living or eating in the same household. People infected with HIV may not show any symptoms for many years, and may first show AIDS-related complex (ARC). This is characterized by chronic swollen lymph glands, weight loss, fatigue, thrush, vaginitis, sweating fever and diarrhoea. ARC is the first stage in the degeneration into full blown AIDS. There is, at this time, no cure for AIDS. Anyone who has had unprotected sex since 1980 is a potential HIV risk.

Akinesia:

Absence or lack of voluntary movement; state of difficulty in initiating movements or changing from one motor pattern to other.

Algolagnia:

Now usually referred to as sado-masochism '

Alias:

A false name used to conceal true identity.

Alibi:

A statement or defense attempting to prove that a subject

suspected of a crime could not have committed the offense.

Alligatoring:

A pattern of deep cracking on the surface of a material that has been burned, indicative of the point of origin of the fire.

Ambivalence:

Presence of strong, often overwhelming, simultaneous contrasting attitudes, ideas, feelings and drives towards an object, person or goal.

Amnesia:

A loss or disturbance of memory (complete or partial, permanent or temporary), attributable to either organic or psychological causes.

Amphetamines:

Drug compounds which have a stimulating effect upon the central nervous system.

Anabolic:

Drug compounds related to the hormone testosterone that stimulate muscle growth and the development of male sex characteristics.

Anhedonia:

Loss of capacity to experience pleasure; seen in depression, and sometimes in schizophrenia.

Anilingus:

Oral—anal sex

Anoacrylate fuming:

A method of developing latent fingerprints in which the fumes of cyanoacrylate ester are discharged from certain types of glues.

Anthropometry:

A system of criminal identification developed by Alphonse Bertillon based on eleven measurements of the human frame.

Anxiety:

An unpleasant emotional state, in which there are feelings of impending danger characterized by uneasiness, tension or apprehension and symptoms of sympathetic overactivity, such as palpitations, tremulousness, difficulty in breathing, dizziness, blurring of vision, sweating, dryness of mouth and increased frequency of micturition.

Apathy:

Lack of feeling or affect, lack of interest or emotional involvement in one's surroundings.

Appeal:

A request that a case be removed from a lower court to a higher court for the purpose of judicial review.

Arch fingerprint:

A fingerprint pattern in which ridges enter from one side, rise in the center, and flow out the other side.

Arrest:

To take a person into custody, by authority of law, for the purpose of answering legal charges.

Arson:

The willful and malicious intentional act of setting fire to property for some improper and illegal motive.

Artificial intelligence:

A computer program which manipulates data and infers conclusions.

Aspermia:

A lack of spermatozoa in semen.

Asphyxia:

Death due to a sudden or gradual cessation of oxygen intake.

Asylum:

The granting governments of sanctuary to suspected criminals individuals; which a nation has the right to grant asylum, a refuge has no legal right to claim it.

At large:

To be free from prison or arrest, applied to escaped prisoners or other hunted fugitives.

At liberty:

Freedom from imprisonment, slavery, or any other form of captivity.

Ataraxics:

A type of tranquilizer often abused by drug addicts. Ataxia.

Ataxia:

A muscular coordination problem that results in unsteady or shaky handwriting.

Atom absorption spectroscopy:

A laboratory technique used to detect elements based on the absorption of light by vaporized atoms.

Atrocity:

Any brutal, cruel, barbaric, evil, or horrifying act.

Attack dog:

A dog trained to attack intruders or threatening individuals on command.

Attack:

To take offensive action against another in an attempt to cause harm.

Attempt:

An overt act that would have resulted in commission of the crime.

Attendant circumstances:

The fact surrounding an event or commission of crime.

Attention:

Part of higher mental functions, that relate to the amount of effort exerted in focusing on certain aspects of an experience or task. When sustained for sufficient length of time, it is termed concentration. Poor attention is characterized by inability to focus on certain aspects of experience or task on hand, also known as distractibility.

Attest:

To make a statement while under oath; to bear witness to.

Attidude arrest:

An arrest made because a police officer does not like someone's behavior.

Attoney-client privilege:

The doctrine that allows communications between an attorney and his client to remain confidential

Attorney:

A person schooled in the law, admitted to practice in a jurisdiction to advise, act on behalf of, and represent people in legal proceedings.

Auburn silent system:

A system of prison discipline begun in 1816 that birth to the workshops of modern prisons and is still practiced, though greatly modified. Through this system, prisoners were confined to their solitary cells at night, but in order to alleviate the monotony of constant confinement and the possibility of insanity or suicide, they were allowed out of their cells each day to world in the prison shop and have meals. During this period, they were forbidden to speak to one another so that criminal ideas could not be promoted. The workshops also made the prison virtually self-sufficient.

Auction pitch:

A card game with four to seven players who are dealt six cards, three cards at a time. The player receiving the first deal determines the trumpet suit, and play continues to his left with the player who wins each trick determining successive trump suits. At the beginning of the game, all players are given seven counters which they must lose in order to win. Loss of a counter occurs when a player successful matches the number of points, or tricks, won with the number that he bid, or proposed to win, at the beginning of each round. If a player bids two tricks and wins two he may remove two counters. If he bids three and only wins two, he must add three counters to his total; a player can only lose the total number of tricks bid even if he were to win more tricks than he had bid, with four being the maximum bid. Betting may take place throughout the game, and the pot may carry over for each hand dealt until a winner is declared or each player may give the winner a predetermined amount for each counter he holds at the game's end.

Autism:

A term introduced by Bleuler to designate a form of thinking, characterized by turning away from reality, uncommunicativeness and an excessive indulgence in fantasy. One of the 4 fundamental symptoms of schizophrenia described by Bleuler. The term is also employed to describe a pervasive developmental disorder of childhood.

Autistic thinking:

A form of thinking driven by inner fantasies, which has no bearing with external realities.

Auto chopping:

The dismantling of the major body components of a vehicle for profit.

Autoerotisism :

Self masturbation

Automated Fingerprint Identification System (AFIS):

Computerized systems which compare fingerprints to a local, state, or federal fingerprint data base to produce identification.

Automatic obedience:

The phenomenon of undue compliance with instructions, seen in catatonic schizophrenia and catatonia due to other causes.

Autopsy:

A posmortm surgical examination to determine cause of death.

B

Baddie:

A criminal with no redeeming characteristics; a bad person.

Bail bond:

And agreement between a defendant and a court which grants the defendant liberty while awaiting trail and guarantees his presence in court for that trail. If the defendant jumps bail and fails to appear for trail the surety forfeits to the state the specified amount of the bond.

Bail:

Money or other security presented to the court to allow the release from custody of a person charged with a crime while guaranteeing his appearance in court at all subsequent proceedings. If he fails to appear, the security is then forfeited.

Bailable action:

One where a defendant may be released from custody only upon a posted bond.

Bailable offense:

An offense for which a prisoner may be eligible for bail.

Bailiff:

An officer of the court who aids in the judicial proceeding.

Ballistics:

The science dealing with the flight behavior of various types of projectiles.

The scientific study of projectiles in flight and, in criminal law, the study of firearms.

Banishment:

The deportation of a person from a country or jurisdiction.

Bank-examiner swindle:

A type of fraud in which a victim is deceived into withdrawing money under the pretense of aiding a bank investigation.

Barbiturates:

Drug compounds which have a depressing or sedative effect on the central nervous system.

BD:

Short for "bondage and discipline".

Beaver:

An American expression for the female pubis area or genitals. The world contains an implied reference to pubic hair.

Behaviour therapy or modification:

A form of psychological treatment aimed at modifying the maladaptive behaviours using principles of learning theory.

Bell- end:

Vulgar expression for glans

Belle indifference:

Apparent lack of concern about disabling symptoms, often a prominent feature of dissociative (conversion) disorders. Historically described as a classical feature of hysteria.

Benzidine test:

A color-reaction tests that indicates the presence of blood.

Blackmail:

Some form of payment obtained from a person to prevent disclosure of information that would bring disgrace or ruin if made public; also referred to as extortion.

Blow-job:

Oral sex

Boner:

Erection

Bookmaker:

An individual who takes and records bets on various events, typically sports activities or horse racing. Often called a "bookie".

Booster devices:

Any object used to assist in a theft, other than the clothing of the thief; typically encountered in shoplifting cases.

Bounty hunter:

A person who tracks criminals with a price on their head; in modern times usually those who have jumped their bail bonds.

Bounty:

The reward that is placed on the head of a criminal and offered to anyone who is able to capture him and brings him to justice.

Bow street runners:

An early group of English criminal investigators who operated from a court located on Bow Street in London.

Box:

Slang term for vagina

Brass:

A prostitute

Bribery:

The giving, offering, or taking of anything, especially money, as an inducement to do something illegal or wrong.

Brown sugar:

(1) A young black woman; (2) excrement

Bugger:

An unnatural act including anal sex and bestiality but excluding oral sex.

Bunco swindles:

Frauds which involve deceit and trickery as the main method of operation.

Burden of proof:

The requirement of a continuous demonstration of guilt, or a proving of each element of a crime against the accused by the prosecution.

Burglary:

The unlawful entering of a legally defined structure with the intent to commit a felony or theft.

Butch/femme:

Lesbian term used in the 1950's indicating butch – a male identified lesbian and femme- a female identified lesbian. The terms went out of use in 1970s but now been revived in the 1990s.

C

C.S.A:
Child sexual abuse

Caning:
A punishment received in prison

Cannabinod:
Any substance which duplicates the mind-altering cannabinol or THC.

Cannabinol:
The active ingredient in marijuana tetrahedro cannabinol or THC

Cannabis indica:
Indian marijuana.

Cannabis american:
U.S. and Canadian grown lowgrade marijuna.

Cannabis mexicana:
Marijuana grown in Mexico.

Cannabis sativa:
The botanical name for marjuana.

Cannabis tea:
Marijuana brewed with tea leaves.

Cannabis:
Marijuna

Cannibal:
One who eats the flesh of other humans.

Cantharides:
The drug "Spanish fly" generally used as an aphrodisiac.

Car clouting:

A suspect method of operation involving the theft of property from a vehicle.

Career criminal:

A criminal perpetrator who has made criminal activity his or her life's work.

Cargo robbery:

The seizure and robbery of loaded tractor trailer trucks by armed offenders; also known as truck hijacking.

Caseload assignment:

Assigning investigative duties without consideration of the nature of a crime; a method that assumes all officers to be generalists equally competent to investigate any offense.

Casino city :

A common nickname for towns where gambling is legal.

Casino:

A card game for two to four players that my be played in teams of two. The objective of casino is to obtain certain cards whose point value will enable a player to win the game. Four cards are dealt face down to each player, two at a time and four cords are dealt to the table face up two at a time. Players pick up the table's cards by pairing cards held in their hand with those on the table combining cards on the table to equal the face value of one they possess, or by adding the value of one card held to one on the table in order to equal a third card held in the hand. The game is played until all the cards are exhausted or a predetermined point total is reached. Points are allotted according to the cards one picks up; e.g. three points for having the most cards two for picking up the ten of diamonds, known as "Big Casino" and one point for picking up the deuce of spades, called "Little Casino".

Castrate:

To remove the testicles of man or animal.

Cat house:

Brothel, prostitute haunt.

Catalepsy:

A generalized condition of diminished responsiveness, usually characterized by trance like states; may occur in organic or psychological conditions, or under hypnosis.

Catatonia:

Immobility with muscular rigidity or inflexibility, and at times excitability seen in schizophrenia.

Chain of custody:

Pertaining to the process by which evidence is handled, transferred, and accounted for between the time of discovery and the disposition of the case.

Chancroid:

A venereal disease exhibiting small septic sores around the sex organs with swelling in the groin.

Check kiting:

A method of suspect operation in which several checking accounts based upon nonexistent funds are opened in the attempt to withdraw funds.

Chicken:

A young person (slang)

Chief justice:

The presiding justice or principle judge of a court.

Child molester:

One who seeks sexual gratification from very young children.

Child pornography:

Material that features chidren performing or involved in acts of sex.

Child snatchning:

The abduction of a child by the parent or grandparent of the child who do not have legal custody of that child.

Child abuse:

Any action or failure to act that endangers or impairs a

child's physical or emotional health and development.

Child abuse:

Any cruelty committed against a child that affect it mentally, morally, or physically.

Circumstantial evidence:

Evidence that does not directly prove the truth of a fact in issue, but that may establish a strong inference as to the truth of that fact; also known as indirect evidence.

Circumstantiality:

A pattern of speech that is indirect and delayed in reaching its goal.

Civil forfeiture:

Government seizure of assets used during a criminal enterprise.

Clanging:

A pattern of speech directed by the sound of a word rather by its meaning. Punning and rhyming may dominate verbal behaviour.

Clipper:

A prostitute who takes a clients money and fails to provide the agreed service.

Clysteromania:

Sexual pleasure obtained from giving or receiving enemas.

Cocaine:

A narcotic extracted from the leaf of the coca bush which produces an intense stimulant effect.

Coercion:

The use of forceful or physically compelling means to obtain information.

Cognitive interview:

An interviewing technique based on questions designed to improve or focus memory recall.

Common law:

Early English judge law that was common to the English people. It formed the basis for subsequent English and American criminal law.

Compulsion:

Unacceptable, repetitive and unwanted urge to perform an act which the patient may carry out.

Computer Aided Identification:

Using computer software to assist victims and witnesses in the identification or facial reconstruction of criminal suspects.

Computer crime:

Frauds that are perpetrated through the misuse of electronic data processing devices.

Concluding investigation:

The final phase of the investigation-terminating an unsuccessful case or preparing a successful case for prosecution.

Concrete thinking:

Thinking characterized by actual things, events and immediate experiences, rather than by abstractions; seen in mistaking a map to be actual terrain; seen in psychosis and young children.

Confabulation:

A disorder of memory in a setting of clear consciousness, characterized by false accounts of past events or personal experiences. The false memories are usually loosely held and have to be evoked.

Confession:

A direct acknowledgment of guilt for the commission of a criminal act.

Confidence swindles:

Frauds or other crimes that are based on deceit or a misrepresentation of facts.

Conflict:

Mental struggle arising from the clash of opposing impulses, drives or demands.

Confusion:

A state of impaired consciousness associated with acute or chronic cerebral organic disease. Clinically it is characterized by disorientation, slowness of mental processes with scanty association of ideas, apathy, lack of initiative, fatigue, and poor attention.

Consciousness, clouding of:

A state of impaired consciousness, representing mild stages of disturbance on the continuum from full awareness to coma.

Consciousness, narrowing (restriction) of the field of:

A form of disorder of consciousness in which the field is restricted to, and is dominated by a small group of ideas and emotions to the virtual exclusion of other content. This condition occurs in extreme fatigue and hysteria.

Consensual crimes:

Offenses that are committed by mutual consent of all parties involved; hence, said to be "victimless" Vice offenses are typical.

Conspiracy:

An agreement between two or more persons to commit a crime in concert.

Contary to law:

1. IIIegal 2. A jury's verdict that contradicts the law the judge gave the jury in this instructions.

Contempt of court:

An intentional act that is intended to obstruct, disobey, hinder, or embarrass a court in its administration of justice, or to lessen its authority or dignity. May be direct, which occurs in or near the court's presence, or indirect, which does not occur in or near the court's presence.

Contempt proceeding:
The trail or hearing conducted to determine whether one has been in contempt of court.

Contempt:
A deliberate disregard, obstruction, or disobedience of public authority.

Continuing offence:
A crime which is perpetrated over a period of time.

Contraband:
Any property crime which is unlawful to possess, produce, transport, export of import.

Contrary to evidence:
Against the evidence or the weight of the evidence.

Contrectation:
An impulse to touch members of the opposite sex in an impolite or indiscriminate way.

Contusions:
Injuries in which the skin is not broken, but blood vessels are ruptured.

Convict labor:
The work that prisoners performs as part of rehabilitation. Some jurisdictions lease this labor to organization outside the prison.

Convict:
A prisoner fund guilty of crime and serving a sentence for its commission

Conviction:
A finding of guilty at the conclusion of a trail, either as the result of a jury's or judge's decision or a guilty plea.

Convictional criminal:
One whose political, social, religious, or ethical beliefs drive him to commit crime.

Coordinated photo series:

A series of crime scene photographs taken in a sequential manner from general to specific subject matter.

Coprophilia:

Sexual intercourse involving excrement.

Coroner:

An official, generally elected, who is legally responsible for investigating deaths within a jurisdiction as determined by law.

Corpus delicti:

The facts constituting or proving the body of a crime, or the necessary elements of a crime which together demonstrate its commission.

Correborate:

To support or confirm known fact or previous testimony with additional or confirming facts or evidence.

Correctional institution:

A place with deals with or house convicted criminals for an extended period; prisons, jails or reformatories.

Corrigible:

Capable of being corrected or changed, especially in reference to a criminal who is capable of being reformed.

Corroborating evidence:

Evidence that supports or confirms evidence already given.

Corroborating witness:

One whose testimony supports statements made by either the victim or the accused.

Corruption:

An act committed by one in an official or fiduciary capacity who unlawfully uses his position to obtain a benefit for himself or another, contrary to his official duties and responsibilities.

Cottage :

A public toilet used by homosexuals as a meeting place.

Counselling:

A process, in which a person facing a problem is helped to clarify and find solutions for the problem.

Crack cocaine:

Nearly pure cocaine which through a heating process is stripped of its hydrochloride granules. After heating, the cocaine is cooled and compressed into dense chunks and typically smoked.

Credit card fraud:

Illegal transactions to defraud individuals or businesses utilizing a personal, altered, or stolen credit card number.

Crime prevention:

The reduction of the commissions of crime, which is the main activity and responsibility of law enforcement agencies.

Crime rate:

The ratio of crimes reported to a specific number of residents.

Crime report:

A complete report on a crime, including witness or victim accounts or the method of operations.

Crime scene:

A location at which a suspected criminal offense has occurred.

Crimes mala prohibita:

Crimes prohibited by statutes because they infrings on other' rights, not because they are necessarily evil by nature.

Crimes, common law:

Criminal acts punished by the force of common law, as opposed to those laws created by statute.

Crime-scene investigator:

An officer specially trained in the processing of physical evidence commonly found at crime scenes.

Crime-scene sketch:

A measured drawing of a scene, showing the relative location of all important items, particularly physical evidence.

Criminal act:

The commission of crime.

Criminal action:

1. A proceeding where the accused is brought to trial, found guilty or not guilty, and sentenced.

Criminal anthropology:

Lombrosian criminology which argues that there are distinguishable types of criminals.

Criminal behavior:

Actions that result in a harm done to society which are punishable by law.

Criminal biopsychology:

The study of psychosomatic personalities of criminals.

Criminal conversation:

Having sexual relations with another other than one's spouse, or having sexual relations with someone else's wife or husband. This is a tort based on adultery, though some states prohibit actions for it.

Criminal etiology:

The area of criminology that studies the biological, physical, psychological and social makeup of an offender to show his behavior as criminal.

Criminal history information:

The information kept on file of one's arrests, convictions, correctional and release records.

Criminal informant:

One who secretly provides information on criminal activities to law enforcement officials.

Criminal insanity:

A mental state that precludes understanding of the criminal nature of the act committed, and/or the inability to determine right from wrong during the commission of the crime.

Criminal intent:

One's state of mind in planning and carrying out a criminal act. Many crimes require general or specific intent for the act to be criminal.

Criminal investigation :

An inquiry involving possible criminal activity based on logic, objectivity, and legal guidelines.

Criminal jurisdiction:

The power of a court to hear and decide criminal cases.

Criminal law:

The body cf law which declares what actions are criminal and prescribes punishment for them, its goal being to prevent harm to society.

Criminal lawyer:

An attorney who specializes in and practices criminal law.

Criminal liability:

One's responsibility for criminal behavior.

Criminal motive:

A state of mind that produces a purpose of a crime. The cause or reason crime falling under criminal law.

Criminal of the upperworld:

A white collar criminal whose social or political status afford him some protection.

Criminal procedure:

Steps taken either to prevent crime or to determine and

punish the guilty party for a crime already committed.

Criminal procedure:

The steps by which a criminal case proceeds, from investigation to the end of the case; the administration of justice.

Criminal process:

A means by which a person is compelled to answer for crime or misdemeanor, e.g., an arrest warrant.

Criminal prosecution:

A proceeding on the public's behalf in a proper court that would convict and punish the accused.

Criminal protector:

One who helps or harbors a felon after the crime's commission.

Criminal psychology:

An application of psychological techniques to studying criminals, criminal behavior, and the treatment and problems of crime.

Criminal sociology:

A science studying societal factors affecting and developing criminal behavior.

Criminal sociopath:

One who dies not comprehend the difference between right and wrong.

Criminal statutes:

Laws enacted by legislative bodies that define, categorize and set punishment for specific crimes.

Criminal syndicalism:

The endorsement of violence or terror for political or economic change, including acts of sabotage to gain control of an industry.

Criminal typologies:

Groupings that criminals can be classified into, e.g. professional criminal, occasional criminal, habitual criminal, conventional criminal, and abnormal criminal

Criminal, the situational:

One who knowingly commits a crime, well aware of that his actions are illegal, and then rationalizes his behavior as being right because of pressing circumstances.

Criminal:

One who has committed as crime Pertaining or connected to criminal laws, penal administration, or that which involves the element to crime.

Criminalism:

Behavior or conduct that is criminal.

Criminalist:

One who is adept at criminal law or criminology.

Criminalistics :

The application of many fields of natural science to the detection of crime.

The scientific investigation of crime.

Criminaloid:

One who is thought to have been born with a criminal disposition.

Criminlistic:

Having a criminal nature.

Criminogenesis:

The source of crime

Criminogenic encephalosis:

A theory that juvenile problems such as indication of future delinquency.

Criminogenic:

That which produces crime, e.g., abuse of drugs and alcohol, living in slums or poverty, overly materialistic views, etc.

Criminologist:

One who studies crime and criminals.

Criminology:

A science which examines and criminals.

Criminosis; crimsons:

A psychoneurotic pattern of behavior marked by criminality.

Criminotechnol:

Using electronic and photographic equipment and techniques to gather evidence and tract down criminals; criminological technology.

Criminotic:

A psychotic or neurotic criminal.

Critical thinking:

A reasoning process characterized by fair-mindedness, intellectual caution, and an openness to question common or assumed beliefs.

Cross- examination:

The courtroom questioning of a witness by an attorney.

Cross-projection:

A method of crime-scene sketching allowing for a three-dimensional view of the scene.

Crunchy or extra crunchy:

Typically identifies the granola type of dyke lesbian often seen by other lesbians as being too politically correct. An American expression.

Cunnilingus:

Oral sex on a woman.

Cunny :

Shortened form of "cunt".

Cunt:

Female genitals.

Cyclical crimes:

Offenses that occur or recur in certain patterns of regularity involving persons, time, or place.

Cypripareunia:

Sexual intercourse with a prostitute.

D

Dactyloscopy :

The study of fingerprints as a means of personal identification.

Dead man:

A convict on death row.

Deadly sin:

A sin that is believed to be fatal to spiritual progress; anger, covetousness, envy, gluttony, lust, pride, and sloth are the seven deadly sins.

Deadly weapon:

Any weapon, device, instrument mater-design is capable of causing great bodily harm.

Deadly weapons per se:

A weapon which through its intended use would ordinarily result in death or great bodily harm.

Death certificate:

A doctor's certificate attesting to the cause of death of a patient under his care. If a person is not under a doctor's care at the time of death, or if the under suspicious circumstances, the local coroner or medical examiner determines the cause of death and issues the certificate.

Death penalty:

The sentence by which life is ended as punishment for a crime or crimes.

Death rattle:

A gurgling or rattling sound made by a dying person as air passes through mucus in the lungs and air passages.

Death trap:

A situation or building that is potentially life- threatening

Death warrant:

An official order to execute a death penalty.

Death watch:

The guard detail that watches over a condemned prisoner, usually, in the days before an execution, to prevent any escape or suicide attempt.

Death:

Permanent cessation of all vital signs and functions; the end of life.

Death's herb:

A drug derived from the belladonna plant.

Deathbed:

That which is accomplished in the last hours one's life, as in a confession.

Deathsman:

An executioner.

Deazingus:

Equipment used in the actual injection of drugs, specifically, a medicine dropper with a needle attached or a hypodermic syringe.

Debauch:

Violent seduction , usually aggravated by assault or ravishment.

Decapitations; decap:

Becheading, sometimes as forms of capital punishment.

Deceit:

A reckless or intentional misrepresentation or deception.

Deception, scientific detection of:

The filed of science that attempts to determine when a lie is being told. Usually through lie detector machines or test.

Decipher:

To decode characters or symbols.

Decision:

The judgment or decree of a court.

Declaration:

A statement, usually not under oath.

Declare out:

To announce oneself out of crime or a gang.

Declasse:

An inmate who has been brought back to a standard prison after a term at a special punishment camp.

Decomposed writing:

A handwriting style where down-stroke and upstrokes are not connected and sometimes not even completed.

Decomposition:

The rotting or decaying of once-living matter.

Decoy:

A persons, usually a police officer, who impersonates a civilian in the hope of attracting a criminal act, e.g., a police-woman who dresses as prostitute in order to arrest men who solicit her for sex.

Deductive reasoning:

Forming a general conclusion prior to having a complete examination based on facts.

Defense wounds:

An attorney who represents the defendant in a legal proceeding.

Defense wounds:

Injuries suffered as a victim attempts to ward off an assailant's blows; typically located on the hands or arms.

Delirium:

An acute organic mental disorder characterized by confusion and altered or fluctuating consciousness due to an alteration of cerebral metabolism.

Delusion:

A false incorrigible belief held firmly despite incontrovertible proof or evidence to the contrary. The belief is out of keeping with reality and with the socially shared beliefs of individual's background and culture. Delusions are of many types, such as persecutary, grandiose, somatic, reference and control.

Denial:

A refusal to admit or acknowledge apparent truth. In psychodynamic theory, denial designates a psychological mechanism of defence by which either a painful experience or an aspect of self is denied.

Density gradient technique:

A laboratory method used to compare and analyze soil evidence through observation of liquid density samples.

Deoxyribonucleic Acid (DNA):

An organic substance found in the chromosomes within the nucleus of a cell containing unique genetic materials.

Dependence:

A cluster of behavioural, cognitive and physiological phenomena that develop after repeated substance use. It includes compulsive urge to take the substance, withdrawal phenomena and tolerance.

Depersonalisation and Derealisation:

In depersonalisation, the individual feels changed in a strange way. He has no feeling for others or himself and this distresses him. This is often associated with derealisation when the environment appears to be unreal and strange. This may occur in depression, schizophrenia, temporal lobe epilepsy and depersonalisation disorder.

Depression:

A mental state characterized by feelings of sadness, loneliness, despair, low self esteem and self reproach. The term refers to a mood that is so characterized. Sometimes, the term is used to describe the depressive illness.

Dildo:

An artificial penis used for masturbation (less common-dildoe)

Direct evidence:

Evidence that directly establishes the main fact of issue, without an inference or presumption; gathered directly from sensory perception.

Direct examination:

The courtroom questioning of a witness by the attorney who called the witness to testify.

Dirt-box:

Slang expression for rectum.

Discharge:

To release from confinement.

Discrimination:

The denying of privileges or rights because of race, age, religion, gender, or national origin

Disfranchise:

To deprive a citizen of rights and privileges e.g. the right to vote.

Dismemberment:

The removal of a person's limbs.

Dismissal:

The dropping of charges by a judicial officer without determining the guilt or innocence of the accused.

Disorderly conduct:

The charge of disturbing the peace or good order of a community. Generally the local statutes are vague about exactly what constitutes such a charge and it has become a catch all used broadly by police.

Disorderly persons:

A general term usually Used in statutes which aplies to people who engages in disorderly conduct.

Disorderly:

Violation of the public peace or the good order of a community

Disorientation:

Impaired awareness of time, place and position of self in relation to other persons.

Disposition:

The judicial decision which ends a trial with an acquittal, dismissal, or a verdict of guilty.

Disqualification:

Deprived of a legal right or function without legal power.

Dissuade:

To advise and convince a person not to commit and act.

Distill:

To heat and then extract the resulting vapors, usually to produce a purer form of the original mixture, a common practice in alcohol and drug production.

Distortion:

An inaccurate photographic result in which true relationships between objects are not achieved.

Disturbance; **disturbance of the peace :**

An act or conduct which interrupts the peace and quiet and the good order of a community.

Disulfiram:

A drug used in the treatment of alcoholics; it causes a severe reaction when alcohol is consumed, and produces nausea, difficulty in breathing, and other discomforts.

Ditch:

(1) To get rid of, to abandon. (2) To abandon accomplices at a crucial moment, e.g., a getaway driver or lookout who flees at the first sight of police, often without warning the inside men.

Doctrine of informer privilege:

A legal principle recognizing that an informant's identity should not be disclosed during a trial if such disclosure would result in retaliation to the informant.

Document examiner:

An expert in the examination of documents, handwriting, typewriting, and associated areas of communication.

Documentary sources of information:

Information of a printed nature or data otherwise recorded and stored in official agency files.

Domestic abuse:

Physical or emotional forms of abuse which take place in a domestic environment.

DP:

Double penetration-indicates that a picture on the Internet is of a woman having intercourse with two men.

Drug abuse:

When narcotics of dangerous drugs are used improperly and/or illegally.

Drug addiction:

A physical or mental state of chronic dependence for a drug substance often characterized by tolerance and withdrawal symptoms.

Duress:

The use of mental compulsion to obtain information usually involving the imposition of restrictions or restrains on physical behavior.

Dying declaration:

A statement given by a victim who has proper knowledge of

his or her imminent death; such statement are exceptions to the hearsay prohibition and are generally allowed into evidence.

Dyke :

A lesbian with dominant or masculine tendencies.

Dysphoria:

An unpleasant mood state characterized by disaffection, dejection, restlessness, anxiety and irritability.

E

Echolalia:

Repetition of another person's words e.g., interviewer's words or phrases.

Echopraxia:

Repetition of another person's actions and movements.

Elation:

A pleasurable affect. It is a jovial mood without any obvious reason, and is associated with increased motor activity. Seen in mania.

Electronic surveillance:

A method of listening to and recording spoken interactions by using devices that gather, amplify, and record communications.

Embezzlement:

A form of larceny where one fraudulently appropriates money or property entrusted to him by another, to his own use or benefit.

Emblaze:

To set on fire.

Embolism:

An obstruction of a capillary or an artery by a blood clot or some other foreign substance traveling in the blood stream, such as globule of fat or an air bubble.

Emboss:

To upraise, as in relief from a surface, e.g., the raised images on a coin.

Embowel:

To remove a person's bowels.

Embracer:

A person who attempts to illegally influence a verdict by tampering with a juror.

Embroidery:

An embellishment or elaboration using decorative and usually fictitious detailed work.

Embryo:

The early stages of human fetus, usually. The first three months of life after conception.

Eme:

Name for the Mexican –American Mafia.

Emission:

The expulsion or ejection of any secretion or other matter from the body, such as urine or semen.

Emmenagogues:

A class of medicines which supposedly have the ability to promote menstruation, and are sometimes used to bring about an abortion.

Emotion:

A complex state of arousal; compounds of widespread physiological changes, heightened perception and subjective experience, tending towards action.

Emotional insanity:

A mental abnormality during which ordinary reasoning abilities are impaired, usually. Caused by excessive emotional responses to a situation or spontaneous violent excitement; a temporary passion causing complete derangement or an impulse which the mind cannot resist.

Emotionally affected victims:

Victims who have experienced direct contact with a criminal suspect and require special considerations during the questioning process.

Empalement:

The ancient punishment of thrusting a sharp pole up the anus.

Employee pilferage:

Theft committed by employees against their place of employment.

Empty handed:

Having obtained or received nothing.

Empty:

To steal from a person emptying them of their money or goods.

EMS technicians:

Paramedics.

Enchain:

To restrain with or as if with chains use.

Enclosure:

A fingerprint identification term describing a ridge line separation which later connects to form an enclosure.

Enfiolade:

To aim and shoot gunfire in a lengthwise direction, or to be in such a position to do so.

Enflame:

To set ablaze. 2. To cause one to become uncontrollable or overly excited.

Enforce:

To effectively carry out or execute, e.g. enforce laws or carry out a judgement. Obtain something by force.

Enforcement:

The carrying out or execution of a law.

Enslave:

To place one under control as if in slavery.

Enslavement:

The subjugation of someone.

Espionage:

1. Spying on another, usually, a country, for the purpose of gathering information 2. Transmitting or losing information pertaining to the national defense of a country with the belief that the information, or lack thereof, will cause injury to that country.

Estoppel:

A prevention or barrier from, making a denial or alleging a fact to the be lie to one's own previous conduct or statement to the contrary.

Ether:

The highly volatile anesthetic gas, ethyl oxide, with can be inhaled, injected into beer, or drunk as a substitute for ethyl alcohol.

Ethyl alcohol:

The sedative, hyponotic drug found in alcoholic beverages whose poisonous properties can cause great disturbance in function.

Etophine:

A derivative of opium, this drug is more than one thousand times stronger than morphine in its sedative, analgesic, and respiratory effects, and is severely regulated by law.

Euphoria:

The feeling of elation and well-being sometimes experienced by drug users, especially during initial experiences with drugs, which are frequently sought and seldom found thereafter.

A pleasurable affect, lesser in degree than elation. There is eightened feeling of well-being without any obvious reason. Seen in mania.

Euphorica:

Any drug that alters the mind, producing a euphoric state.

Euroterro:

A European terrorist.

Euthanasia:

A homicide intended to put a sick person out of misery; a mercy killing.

Evade (for):

A prisoner who has attempted escape.

Evade:

To elude capture or detection by ingenuity.

Evaluation:

An appraisal of value.

Evasion:

The fact of eluding or evading.

Evidence, circumstantial:

Testimony not based on actual knowledge or observation of the fact in question, or by any indirect evidence from which reasonable deduction may be drawn to prove the claimed hypothesis.

Evidence, hearsay:

Evidence not derived from the personal knowledge of a witness but rather from what he has heard others say. In some jurisdictions, testimony to any out-of-court statement, event the witness's own, is considered hearsay. This evidence is generally inadmissible, although there are several exemptions dying declaration.

Evidence, inculpatory:

Incriminating evidence with tends to establish a person's involvement in a crime.

Evidence, medical:

Evidence with is provided to the court by a licensed medical doctor. The evidence given can be either in the form of a document, if the physician is unable to attend the proceeding, or as testimony during the trial. This expert witness can testify to matters of fact as well as opinion concerning the case.

Evidence, rules of:

The rules of law governing the admissibility of evidence and determining what weight, if any, should be given to specific testimony, documents, or objects.

Evidence:

Any type of proof, which when legally presented during a trial, is admitted into the official record for the review of judge and jury.

Evidence:

Testimony of witnesses, concrete objects, exhibits, documents, records, or other data pertaining to the issue at trail. 2. The proof on which a judgment is based.

Evidentiary fact:

Facts which are needed to determine the ultimate facts.

Evil eye:

A glance or eye believed capable of causing harm. 2. One who possesses such a look or eye.

Evil minded:

Having thoughts or a demeanor that is evil in nature.

Evil:

That which causes or brings wrongdoing, harm, or misfortune. 2. Causing or manifesting harm.

Evildoing:

An action or act of an evil nature use.

Exaction:

The act of compelling a payment or reward for services, under the guise of official authority, when no payment is actually due.

Examination:

An inspection, interrogation, search, or investigation.

Examining trail:

A hearing to determine if there is probable cause for a person to be bound over to a grand jury.

Excitement:

A state of psychomotor overactivity.

Exclusionary rule:

Legal principle which excludes evidence from trial which has been obtained illegally by the authorities.

Exculpatory:

Evidence which exonerates or clears a person of blame or legal guilt.

Exhibitionism:

The exposure of the sex organ, under other than conventionally lawful circumstances, for sexual gratification; commonly known as indecent exposure.

Exhumation:

Disinterment of a body from a tomb or grave.

Expert testimony:

Testimony given during a judicial proceeding by an individual who by virtue of education, training, and experience has knowledge or skill in a particular field beyond the knowledge of the average person.

Explosive tagging:

A technique in which minute coded particles are added to explosives during their manufacture for future identification purposes.

External perception:

Conditions that are not intrinsic to an individual, but which affect his or her ability to acquire and relate information.

Extradition:

A legal procedure by which a person who commits a crime in one jurisdiction and flees to another can be arrested in the second jurisdiction and returned to the original jurisdiction to be tried for the charge.

Eyewitness identification:

An identification , usually of another person, by a person who witnessed a criminal act.

F

Facetiae:

Euphenism used by libraries and publishers for pornography.

Fanny :

(1) vagina; (2) behind (US).

Fear:

A primitive, intense emotion in the face of threat, real or imagined, which is accompanied by physiological reactions resulting from arousal of the sympathetic nervous system and by defensive patterns of behaviour associated with avoidance, flight or concealment.

Fellatio:

Oral sex on a male.

Felonious homicide:

The killing of human being without excuse or justification.

Felony murder:

A common law doctrine classifying any unintentional death which occurs during the commission of a felony as murder. Today the requirements for felony murder vary greatly by jurisdiction.

Felony:

A crime more serious than a misdemeanor, generally punishable by incarceration in a state or federal prison for at least one year.

A criminal act of graver consequence than those identified as misdemeanors, usually punishable by more than one year of imprisonment to by execution.

Femicide:

The homicide of a woman.

Femme fatale:

A woman who seductively lures men into dangerous situation.

Femme:

Butch/female.

Fence :

A buyer and seller of stolen property.

Fetch:

To steal

Feticide:

The criminal destruction of a human fetus; an illegal abortion.

Fetish(-ism):

An unbalanced sexual preoccupation with a particular body part, feature, item of clothing or type of material.

Fetish:

Any non sexual object, e.g., a foot, that must be present or fantasized about for sexual gratification to be achieved by the person who has a fixation for the object.

Fetishism:

A sexual perversion involving an inanimate object, or a specific body part, as the sole stimulator for sexual gratification.

An abnormal condition in which one is sexually aroused and satisfied by displacing erotic interests with a non sexual object.

Fetter:

To restrain; to bind with shackles or chains.

Feud:

A long-standing or prolonged quarrel or hostility between different parties, esp. fighting between families or clans with vengeful violence.

Fiction of law:

An assumption that that which is possible is true, even if its is false.

Fiction:

A story that is invented.

Fingerprint classification:

A file-and-retrieval system in which various numbers and letters are assigned to fingerprints in a multistep process.

Fingerprint:

The identifying marks in the epidermal surface of the fingertip, which can be traced scientifically to an individual.

Finish:

To kill or dispose of completely.

Fire bomb:

An incendiary device, used for destroying structures, disabling armored vehicles, or terrorizing.

Firearms Acts:

Criminal statutes covering the illegal possession, sale, and use of firearms and ammunition.

Firearms:

Weapons in which a gunpowder explosion propels a projectile.

First degree murder:

Modern criminal statutes generally define murder as "first degree" or second degree". First degree murder typically includes those committed after premeditation; felony murders are also commonly included in this classification.

First Aid:

Emergency medical care given to someone before regular medical care is available

Fisting:

Sexual arousal involving the insertion of the whole fist to

the forearm into the vagina or anus.

Flagellomania:

Erotic pleasure from whipping or being whipped.

Flashing:

Indecent exposure.

Flight of ideas:

Verbal skipping from one idea to other. The ideas appear to be continuous but are fragmentary and determined by chance or temporal associations.

Footprint:

An impression left by one's foot.

Forcible trespass:

The taking or damaging of the personal property of another by force.

Forcible entry:

Entering or taking possession of space or and against the will of those with the legal right of possession.

Forcible rape:

The unlawful act of forcing a person to participate in or submit to sexual intercourse.

Forensic anthropologist:

Specialists, generally anthropologists, skilled at providing investigative clues from decomposed human remains.

Forensic ballistics:

The scientific study of projectiles in flight; the study of firearms.

Forensic medicine:

The muse of chemicals or of medicine to deduce case or time of death or for other legal purposes.

Forensic odontology:

The use of teeth and / or dental records for the purpose of

identifying physical remains or the source of bit wounds, or obtaining criminals evidence.

Forensic pathologist:

A physician who specializes in the study of changes in body tissues as a result of disease or death and the impact of such evidence on legal cases, typically homicides. This person may work with the coroner in determining the cause of death.

Forensics:

The art or study of argumentation and formal debate used in courts of law and debate.

Forfeit:

Something which is taken from someone for a crime or offense. To have some property or right confiscated for a crime or offense.

Forfeiture:

Losing the right to something because of error, default, or as a penalty for certain crimes.

Forge:

To create a fraudulent copy of something with the intent of substituting the copy for the original for fraudulent or deceitful purposes.

Forger:

A counterfeiter or one who alters or fabricates documents or signature.

Forgery:

The international duplication or replication of something; the creation of a new work represented as the work of another. Something that has been forged.

The making or alteration of a document without authority and with the intention to defraud.

Form niveau:

The aesthetic measure of a handwriting sample.

Formaldehyde:

A pungent, irritating, colorless gas used in the preservation of organic matter or as a disinfectant.

Fornication:

Unlawful sexual intercourse between a man and woman who are unmarried.

Frame:

Evidence which has been manufactured or distorted to make an innocent man appear guilty.

Fratricide:

The killing of a sister or brother.

Fraud:

Any deceitful action in which a person distorts, withholds, misrepresents, or fabricates information in order to injure another person or deprive him of a property or right.

Fraudulent conversion:

Receipt of another's money or property and its diversion for one's personal use or for the use of someone other than the rightful owner.

Fraudulent:

Designed to carry out a fraud; based on fraud, tainted, characterized by fraud.

Freak out:

To go out of one's mind, whether from alcohol, drugs, temporary insanity, or shock.

Freak:

A frequent user of narcotics.

Freaking freely:

Behaving spontaneously and without inhibition under the influence of LSD.

Freddy:

A pill of the stimulant ephedrine.

Freebase:

A chemical or heating process that frees base cocaine from its hydrochloride powder.

Freedom of Information Acts:

A federal law providing a formal request procedure for public access to government records.

Frig:

Masturbate.

Frotteur(-ism):

A male who obtains sexual satisfaction by rubbing up against a woman-often her buttocks.

Fuck:

Slang expression for sexual intercourse.

Fugue:

A flight or wandering, of short or long duration, from familiar surroundings in a state of altered consciousness, usually followed by partial or complete amnesia for the event. A type of dissociation state.

Futures research:

Research activities which seek to accurately predict investigative trends, incidents, and organizational policy in anticipation of future realities.

G

G.L.B.:
Short for "gay, lesbian, bisexual", on the Internet.

Gam:
Gamahuche or gamaruche-oral sex.

Gas chamber:
A room where prisoners are executed with poisonous gas.

Gas chromatograph:
A device that measures a drunk diver's intoxication level.

Gas pistol:
A weapon that silently fires lethal cyanide gas.

Gassing:
A gas chamber execution.

Gavel:
A mallet used by a judge to bring silence to a court proceeding or to announce a recess or end of a trial.
A sucker, a swindle victim.

Gay:
Homosexual- a term intended to show a happy and positive attitude to homosexuality.

Gerbilling:
A peculiar practice developed by homosexuals on the West Coast of America which involves the placing of a live gerbil (sometimes enclosed in a condom) into the anal orifice.

Glans:
The head or tip of the penis.

Golden rain (slang):
Urine.

Gonads:

Seed producing sexual organs, i.e. testicles and ovaries.

Gonorrhoea:

The most common from of venereal disease in tropics. It can be spread by vaginal, anal, or oral intercourse. It has poor survival outside the body and is unlikely to be spread other than sexually. However, anal infection in a woman does not indicate anal intercourse as it can spread along the perineum. In addition it can be spread by contact with an infected towel.

Goose:

Either anal sex or to pinch someone's bottom.

Grand theft:

A form of theft classified as a felony on the basis of amount of property loss or circumstances of the act.

Grandiosity:

Exaggerated notions of capacities, possessions and esteem, which may be ideational or to delusional proportions. Seen in mania, schizophrenia and organic brain disorders.

Grid search:

A crime scene search method in which searchers process the area in a crisscross fashion; often used for large outdoor scenes.

Group home:

A residence for adult or juvenile offenders. Who are free to come and go, for those who are not ready for parole or who need to readjust to the community after imprisonment.

Groups therapy:

Psychotherapeutic treatment by one or more trained professionals who treat a group of patients simultaneously, using the group setting for peer feedback and social pressure to bring about change in individuals.

Grower:

One who grows marijuana.

Gruel:

To wear down or exhaust one by relentless questioning or severe punishment or to die, usually by hanging.

Guard:

One who is employed to keep an eye on another, e.g. a prison guard.

To protect or watch over someone or something To keep a close watch over so as to prevent escape or wrongdoing.

Guardian:

A court appointed caretaker, usually one who cares for a child or mentally incompetent person.

Guilt:

The condition of having violated the law.

Guilty but mentally ill:

A verdict available in some trails involving an insanity defense, a verdict meaning that psychiatrists will examine the prisoner before he goes to prison, and if he needs treatment, he will be sent to a mental health institution.

Guilty plea:

An official statement of guilt that the defendant makes in court, but only after he has been advised of his rights.

Guilty verdict:

Official decision of a jury who has found the defendant guilty.

Guilty:

The word a defendant uses of his plea when he admits that he committed the crime with which he is charged. A term that conveys a jury's verdict that the defendant committed the crime with which he was charged. Having been found to have committed a crime or violation of law.

Gun records:

A division in a government agency which contains files which the serial numbers and makes of all registered weapons and information relating to permits to carry a concealed weapon.

Gunpowder:

A powder used as charge for guns or explosives consisting of charcoal, potassium nitrate, and sulfur.

Gunslinger :

One noted for his ability and speed in using a gun,

Gunsmith:

A craftsman who makes or designs guns.

Gypsy:

A member of a group of wandering fortunetellers who pretend to be descended from the ancient Egyptians, known for their knowledge of science; gypsies offer to tell fortunes and often rob or swindle the gullible.

H

Habeas corpus:

Shortening of habeas corpus ad subjiciendum.

Habeas corpus acts (Lat):

The various act involving habeas corpus and subjiciendum. The original act was an English statute. Similar laws have been enacted throughout the world and are considered the primary constitutional guarantee of personal freedom.

Habeas corpus ad subjiciedum (Lat):

Literally. You have the body. A court order most often used to determine if a person is being unlawfully detained or imprisoned. Habeas corpus is not used to test a prisoner's guilt or innocence.

Habeas corpus and deliberandum et recipeindum (Lat):

A court order authorizing the removal of a person from custody in one jurisdiction for prosecution in another.

Habeas corpus and satisfaciendum (Lat):

In England, a court order desired by a plaintiff to brings a convicted prisoner to a superior court where an order of execution prisoner to a superior court where an order of execution may be obtained.

Habeas corpus and testificandum (Lat):

Literally, "You have the body to testify." A court order used to bring a prisoner to court to testify.

Habeas corpus:

See Writ of habeas corpus.

Habemus optimum testem, confitentem reum (Lat):

Literally, "we have the best witness", used to describe a person who confesses to committing the crime with which he is charged.

Habes corpus ad prosequendum (Lat):

A court order that takes effect when it is necessary to remove a prisoner from one area to be prosecuted in the jurisdiction where his alleged offense occurred.

Habit forming drug:

Any drug that may produce a physical or psychological addiction, psychosis, personality changes, increased tolerance, or feeling of euphoria.

Habit forming:

Leading to addition.

Habit smoker:

One who is addicted to smoking opium.

Habit, kick a:

To withdraw from the additive use of a drug and consequently suffer physical and psychological symptoms.

Habit:

A physical or psychological dependence on drugs or alcohol.

Habitual criminal:

A repeat offender who is subject to more severe penalties in most states than a first-time offender. A person with a long criminal record who is under frequent police surveillance and is arrested on suspicion.

Habitual drunkenness:

A condition in which a drinker readily and frequently gets intoxicated, usually indicative of alcoholism.

Habituation:

A psychological addition to drugs or alcohol. A condition caused by the frequent use of a drug, usually Marijuana or cocaine. It causes a person to want to continue its use for the sense of well – being it creates, usually without wanting to increase the dosage and not resulting in physiological withdrawal symptoms. This conditions was defined by the World Health Organization of the United Nations in 1957.

Hacksaw:

A fine-toothed saw that is able to cut through tough materials such as metal.

Hadamaki:

A baggy Japanese sweater used to hide valuables.

Hag:

A female evil spirit.

Hagrid:

To torment or harass.

Halifax law:

The unauthorized trial and execution of a person, especially by a lynch mob or vigilantes. It is named for the Halifax parish in England, where unauthorized justice was rendered against suspected thieves.

Hallucination:

A temporary distortion of objective reality, usually caused by taking mind- altering drugs.

A false sensory perception, occurring in the absence of an adequate external stimulus. Can occur in any of the five senses. Seen in psychotic disorders.

Hallucinogen:

A natural or synthetic drug that distorts a user's perception of objective reality and may cause brain damage through repeated use, e.g. LSD or mescaline.

Hallucinogenic drug:

Drugs which cause one to experience distortion of reality or wild dreams.

Hallucinogenic mushrooms:

Any mushrooms soaked in hallucinogenic chemicals.

Hallucinogenic:

Causing hallucination.

Hallucinogens:

Drug substances, both natural and synthetic, that distort

the perception of objective reality.

Haloperidol:

A non-addictive drug used to relieve withdrawal symptoms. Usually from methadone and heroin addiction.

Handmark:

A palmprint.

Hard-on:

An erection.

Hashish :

A derivative of the cannabis (marijuana) plant obtained from leaves that produce a resin having the most powerful euphoric properties.

Hate crimes:

Crimes that are motivated by a particular victim's race, region, caste, religion, sexual orientation, or ethnicity.

Hazing:

A organized form of harassment, often humiliating or painful, commonly used as part of initiation into a fraternity or club

H-caps:

Heroin capsules.

Hearing:

A court proceeding that is somewhat less formal than a trial. Arguments, witnesses, and evidence are presented to a judge or administrative body. An initial court proceeding in criminal law presenting the accused party and witnesses for the defense.

Hears:

A coffin. Funeral bier.

Hearsay:

Testimony not based on the personal knowledge of the witness, but on information obtained from others. The hearsay statement may be oral, written, or even non- verbal conduct, and typically does not describe what the witness knows personally. Hearsay is generally inadmissible, but there are many exceptions, e.g., an official police report, or the testimony of co-conspirators after a conspiracy is established.

Hemp:

The marijuna plant, Cannabis sativa. Marijuna, esp. in a cigarette.

Hepatitis:

An inflammation of the liver, often caused by the use of contaminated needles during intravenous drug use. Frequent symptoms include jaundice, fever, and chills.

Hepatitis-B:

An infection which may be passed sexually, very highly infective.

Heroin:

An extremely physically – addictive, illegal drug derived from the acetylation of morphine or from opium. Heroin is usually ground into fine white or chunky brown powder and injected or smoked by users. Unlike morphine and a few other harsh narcotics, heroin has no legitimate medicinal functions.

An opiate derivative chemically converted from morphine.

He-she:

A male transvestite dressed to look like a female hooker.

Hesitation marks:

Minor cuts found close to a major wound, usually Found in suicide victims. These cuts are believed to result from personal indecision or a test of the instrument's efficiency.

Wounds which indicate the testing of an edged weapon prior to an attempted or completed suicidal cutting.

Homicidal:

Relating to homicide. Prone to homicide.

Homicide stab wounds:

The fatal and superficial wounds found on a corpse. Wounds found on the arms and hands usually suggest that the victim tried to fight back.

Homicide by misadventure:

The accidental killing of another person while engaged in a lawful activity.

Homicide by necessity:

The legal killing of another that is required by law, e.g. capital punishment.

Homicide per infortunium:

The killing of a person in self –defense during a sudden attack, in which the killed had no other reasonable option, a type of excusable homicide.

Homicide reckless:

In some states, the criminal killing of another person through willfully careless behavior.

Homicide, negligent:

The criminal killing of another through negligence.

Homicide, culpable:

The criminal killing of another with varying degrees of guilt.

Homicide, excusable:

The slaying of another human being through and accident or self-defence.

Homicide, felonious:

Homicide that is a felony, either murder or manslaughter.

Homicide, justifiable:

The intentional killing of another but without any evil intent. e.g., in the case of capital punishment or a availing top prevent a felony.

Homicide, vehicular:

The unlawful killing of another through the reckless operation of motor vehicle, usually a car, truck or motorboat, etc.

Homicide:

The killing of a human by another human; may be criminal or authorized by law.

The killing of one human being by another. Homicide is not always a crime, e.g., in the case of capital punishment. Murder, manslaughter and negligent homicide are unlawful homicide. There are no degree of murder in common law, but statutes often categorize murder as "first" or "second degree".

Homosexuality:

An erotic attraction to, or sexual preference for, a member of the same sex.

Hooker:

American term for a prostitute.

Hypnosis:

A state of complete physical relaxation and intense mental concentration in which the subject's suggestibility is maximized.

Hypnotism:

The process of introducing a mental state that sometimes causes a person to remember traumatic events. The patient is subject to the will of the inducer but will not perform actions he would never consider in a fully conscious state.

Hypodermic injection:

An injection made beneath the skin.

Hypodermic needle:

A needle attached to a syringe for injection under the skin.

Hypodermic syringe:

A tube like instrument containing a drug to be injected through a needle into or beneath the skin.

Hypodermic:

An apparatus (needle and syringe) used to inject a substance into a vein. An injection into a vein or under the skin.

Hypomania:

A mild form or the early stage of a mania.

Hypothesis:

An assumption or explanation for an occurrence which is then tested for its validity.

I

Ideas of reference:

Morbid interpretation of indifferent, external phenomena as carrying personal and usually noxious significance. They tend to occur in sensitive individuals at times of stress and fatigue, and also in psychotic disorders.

Illegal arrest:

An arrest made without sufficient evidence that a crime has been committed or one made without the necessary warrant.

Illegal entry:

To enter a country at a wrong time or place, or to evade immigration or enter by way of fraud.

Illegal:

Not authorized by the law or against the law.

Illegitimate:

A person or thing not sanctioned by law.

Illicit:

Illegal unethical, or immoral

Ill-treatment:

Cruel or improper treatment of another

Illusion:

A mistaken, distorted, or perverted image or impression caused by the imagination of the observer, not by a defect in any of the organs of sense.

A misinterpretation of a real stimulus. Can occur in a normal person, as well as in morbid states.

Illy-whacker:

A confidence decay or feebleness of there mind. It varies

in degreed from mere eccentricity to almost total madness. Imitation.

Imbecility:

An advanced decay or feebleness of the mind. It varies in degrees from mere eccentricity to almost total madness.

Imitation:

Something which is produced or made in likeness of the original; a counterfeit copy.

Immediate cause:

The final act in a chain of events or causes; what which directly produces the results or events without further intervention, not necessarily the same as the proximate cause.

Imminent danger:

One of the essential elements of a self-defense plea in a homicide case, this is a person's belief of impending peril, with no reasonable way of escape except to meet force with force.

Imminent peril:

A position of danger where death or bodily injury is reasonably certain.

Imminently dangerous article:

An object that is reasonably certain to put life or lim at risk.

Immoral:

Conflicting with general standards of moral behavior. Obscene, without redeeming social value.

Immunity:

Exemption from prosecution, generally for information or testimony of value to the state.

Impaired physician:

A doctor who is handicapped by an addiction to alcohol or other drugs.

Impeach:

To dispute, contradict, deny disparage, malign, denounce, accuse indict, charge, sue, challenge; e.g. to impeach a witness is to challenge his credibility.

Impeachment:

The bringing of criminal charges against a public officer before a quasi political court, e.g., a legislative body.

Impersonate:

To portray or assume the character of another.

Implicate:

To connect a person with an illegal act.

Implied consent:

A presumption that consent has been given based upon certain signs or actions, or by lack of action or silence.

Importer:

One who imports dangerous drugs.

Impost-taker:

One who lends money to gamblers at extremely high interest rates.

Impound:

To confine someone or place in the custody of the law.

Impoundment:

Placement of a person in custody.

Imprison:

To confine a person, usu, in a prison.

Imprisonment:

The act of confining a person.

Impulsiveness:

Sudden motor activity with no obvious premeditation.

In propria persona:

Translates to " in one's own proper person," and means to be without the aid of an attorney in a legal matter.

Incendiary fire:

An intentionally set fire in which the means of ignition varies accordingly to the skill and motive of the arsonist.

Incest:

Sexual intercourse between individuals of any age too closely related to marry.

Incoherence:

A severe form of thought and speech disorder in which the prominent features are distortion of grammar, unexplained shifts from topic to topic, and lack of logical connection between parts of speech.

Incriminating circumstance:

A fact or occurrence collateral to the commission of a crime which tends to show that the crime has been committed or that a specific person committed it.

Incriminating admission:

An acknowledgement of facts which tend to establish guilt.

Incriminating evidence:

Fact which tend to establish guilt. Either by themselves or with other evidence.

Incrimination:

The act of implicating oneself or another in a criminal charge.

Incriminatory statement:

Any statement which tends to establish guilt, either by itself or along with other evidence.

Incriminatory:

Tending to incriminate.

Inculpate:

To accuse, or to involve one in crime or the guilt of crime.

Inculpatory evidence:

Evidence which is incriminating, as it tends to establish guilt.

Inculpatory:

A general term that covers a number of offenses, including indecent exposure and public indecency.
Type of testimony or other evidence which tends to, or is intended to, establish guilt.

Indecent assault:

The act of a male person's taking indecent liberties against a female without her consent and against her willing it, but with no intent to commit rape.

Indecent exposure:

The criminal act of exposing one's sexual parts to another in public.

Indemnification for errors of justice:

Compensation for those who have been wrongly convicted and imprisoned.

Indepth investigation:

A phase of the investigative process which follows up initial leads developed during the preliminary investigation and attempts to open new areas of inquiry.

Indeterminate sentence:

A prison sentence, authorized by statute, where the court imposes the minimum and maximum length of the incarceration, e.g., three to five years. The actual date of release is determined by an administrative board, usually based on the inmate's conduct while in prison.

Indian hay:

Marijuana which comes from Indian hemp.

Indian hemp:

Plants from which marijuana and hashish are obtained.

Indict:

To charge with a crime

Indictable:

Type of action or deed that may lead to an indictment.

Indictment:

A formal written statement charging a person with a criminal offense. The charge must then be proven at trial.

A written document charging one or more persons is a criminal offense.

Indictor:

A person who cause another to be indicted. The person indicted who causes another to be indicated. The person indicted is sometimes referred to as the indictee.

Indirect evidence:

Evidence which does not prove the fact or facts in question, but from which inferences can be made and presumptions drawn to prove the hypothesis claimed.

Inducement:

The motive that leads to a crime, or the attraction that lures one towards a crime.

Inductive reasoning:

A thinking process in which a conclusion is reached only after all particular facts are gathered and considered.

Industrial revolution:

An economic phase characterized by intense industrial development within urban areas and related population shifts to the cities.

Inebriate:

A habitual drunk.

Infamous:

Having been found guilty of committing a crime which brings infamy.

Infamy:

An evil reputation resulting from some thing blatantly malicious, wrong, or startling. An evil or criminal act which is well-known and extreme in nature.

Infancy:

The status of a person who is under the age of legal majority. In common law children under fourteen are presumed to be without criminal capacity.

Infanticide:

The killing of a newborn baby.

Inference:

A logical method of reasoning in which facts already proven or admitted are used to establish subsequent fact.

Informant file:

A repository for information pertaining to informants – names, addresses, photographs, fingerprints, and so forth.

Informants with ulterior motives:

Individuals who provide information to the police for self-seeking motivations other than financial gain.

Information:

A document prepared by the prosecuting attorney setting forth the charge against the defendant.

Inhalants:

Controlled or noncontrolled chemicals that emit fumes taken into the body to achieve an altered mental state.

Inhibition of thought:

Slowing down of progress of thought. Seen in depression.

Injection kit:

Materials typically carried by an intravenous drug addict necessary to inject narcotics into the bloodstream, or muscles.

Inquest:

A legal inquiry, often by a jury, into a certain matter, corner or medical examiner's inquiry unto as certain death.

Inquiry:

The systematic investigation into a matter, e.g., an unexplained death.

Inquisition:

An inquest or inquiry.

Insane:

Displaying inanity, psychotic or crazed.

Insanity as a bar to execution:

A provision which bars the execution of criminals condemned to die for their crimes if it is found that they were insane at the time of the crime or have since become insane.

Insanity, partial:

An unsound mental condition which always exists in one, but is only occasionally apparent.

Insanity:

Any mental illness which prevents one from attaining the required mental capacity to be held responsible for one's action.

Insight:

Degree of awareness about one's illness, one self.

Inspect:

To thoroughly look into or investigate a matter.

Institution:

An establishment or location of an organization or group of people, e.g., prison.

Institutional capacity:

The number or inmates a prison is designed or allowed to house.

Institutionalize:

To place a person in the hand or care of an institution.

Instrument:

The member of a pick pocketing gang who actually picks the pockets.

Insubstantial:

Having a lack of substance or material nature. e.g., evidence which does not carry much weight.

Insurance crimes:

Arson for profit, murder to collect life insurance, and all other crimes committed to collect insurance.

Insurrection:

A combined resistance of citizens to their government; a rebellion.

Intelligence community:

The intelligence –gathering organizations in any country.

Intelligence investigation:

A law enforcement investigation where the immediate goal is not arrest or prosecution.

Intelligence:

Law enforcement function concerned with gathering, evaluating, and disseminating data related to criminal activity.

An agency or department of an organization involved in the gathering and dissemination of information e.g., police intelligence.

The general mental ability to overcome difficulties in new situations.

Intelligence-gathering:

Recording, collecting, analyzing, and disseminating information, for national security, military, or law enforcement use.

Intent- to kill murder :

Murder resulting from a premeditated or unpremeditated intention of killing another, whether the intended victim or someone else is killed. If a person shoots at someone intending to kill him, but ends up killing another, the crime is still murder because there was an intention to commit such a crime.

Intent to kill:

An element of certain aggravated assault and battery cases

that requires proof of the intent to kill as well as other elements as assault and battery. Other elements include assault with intent to rape, rob, commit mayhem or do great bodily injury.

Intent-to-serious-bodily- injury murder:

One is considered guilty of murder when he intends to cause serious or great bodily injury to another but the result is death, even when the intention was only to cause harm and not death.

Inter:

To place a corpse in a grave or tomb.

Intercept:

To seize or prevent the progress of, e.g., arresting a criminal.

Inter-crural intercourse:

Intercourse simulated or accidentally achieved by rubbing the penis between the partner's legs.

Interfered with :

Euphemism for rape.

Interior intrusion enunciator:

A type of burglar alarm.

Internal perceptions:

Factors intrinsic to witnesses that influence perception and observation.

Internal security:

The branch of law and government in charge of protecting a country from subversive activity,

International terrorism:

Terrorist acts by groups or individual that are not restricted to one country.

Interrogate:

To ask questions systematically and formally.

Interrogation:

A law enforcement questioning procedure involving an individual suspected as a law violator.

The act of formally and systematically questioning someone.

Interrogator:

One who asks questions during an interrogation.

Interstate transportation:

Movement between two or more states within a country.

Interstate:

Between two or more state.

Interview:

A communication involving two or more people for the purpose of obtaining information.

Investigative ethics:

The study of rightful and wrongful human conduct as it applies to the actions of criminal investigators.

Investigative research:

The application of scholarly methods of data acquisition as it applies to the investigative process.

Iodine fuming:

A technique in which crystals of iodine are exposed to a heat source for the purpose of revealing latent fingerprints.

Irritability:

An undue state of excitability, annoyance, impatience or anger. May occur in states of fatigue and chronic pain and as a symptom in a wide range of psychiatric disorders.

J

Jackpot:

A Game of poker where a pair of jacks or a better hand is needed to open betting. A large prize to be won from the accumulation of stakes unclaimed or won in previous games; the winnings of a poker game which no one won and are carried over to the next game. An arrest by police. The top prize, usually on a slot machine.

Jail bait (slang) :

An attractive girl under the age of consent.

Jerk-off (slang) :

Masturbate.

Joy rider:

A drug user, usually on an occasional basis. An amateur car thief, one who steals just to take are ride.

Joyriding:

The stealing of a motor vehicle for pleasure rather than profit motives.

Judgement:

A critical evaluation of the relation between objects, situations, concepts or terms. A prepositional statement of these relations.

Jugs:

Slang expression for breasts.

Jurisdiction:

A geographical area of legal authority within which an individual, agency, or court operates.

Jury -box:

The enclosed place in the courtroom, usually raised, where the jury sits during the course of the trial

Jury:

A body of individuals, legally selected and sworn to consider matters of fact during a trial, that render a verdict of guilty or not guilty.

A group of citizens selected and sworn in to hear evidence and decide the truth of a certain legal matter. The system may not exist everywhere.

Justice:

Administration and enforcement of just principles and regulations, especially by those determined to provide an impartial view of what is right or wrong.

Justifiable homicide:

A killing in self-defence, where danger of death or serious bodily injury exists. An execution ordered by the state. The act of killing by an officer of the law in the prevention of a crime or unlawful escape.

Justifiable:

That which is able to be justified or defended.

Justification:

A lawful or just reason to act or not to act. It is an acceptable excuse for the action taken or not taken, and the ability to justify one's actions to a curt by the use of supporting evidence.

Justinian code:

The code of laws which is the basis for much of modern European law, named for the early Roman emperor Justinian-I who issued it.

Juvenile adjudication:

The final decision of a juvenile court.

Juvenile courts:

The courts that have jurisdiction over juvenile delinquents and dependent and neglected juveniles.

Juvenile delinquency:

Any criminal or anti-social acts committed by a youth who

has not reached the legal age of adulthood.

Juvenile delinquent:

A person who has yet to reach the legal age of adulthood who commits criminal or anti-social acts.

Juvenile gang:

A group of minors engaged criminal acts.

Juvenile office:

A police officer whose duties include detecting, prosecuting, and caring for juvenile delinquents.

Juvenile record:

The official records of a juvenile. including court proceedings and detention or referral records.

Juvenile:

A person yet to reach the age where he could be treated as an adult for the purposes of criminal law. The age varies with jurisdiction.

K

Keister:

U.S. slang. Lit: A bag for tools or satchel, also "the area upon which one sits", the buttocks.

Kicback; kick back:

The part of the loot, profit, or pay which is illegally given to the police or other officials to avoid prosecution, or as a reward for a job or a contract. Stolen property which is returned for one reason or another, usually to avoid prosecution.

Kick a habit:

To end a narcotics or alcohol addiction.

Kidnapper:

One who abducts human beings, usually to hold for ransom.

Kidnapping:

The criminal act of forcibly abducting another human.

Kill off :

To kill or destroy completely or large numbers.

Killing by misadventure:

The accidental killing of one human being by another while the killer is engaged in some lawful act, without criminal carelessness or reckless conduct.

Killing power:

The potency of a bullet or gun, or some other deadly weapon.

Killing:

The act of murder. Large gambling wining.

Kleptomania:

A persistent neurotic impulse to steal, frequently without economic motive.

Knowingly and willfully:

With conscious knowledge and decision.

Knowledge:

The state of understanding, comprehending. Knowing.

K-Y jelly:

Trade name of a water soluble lubricant used to facilitate sexual intercourse.

L

La Cosa Nostra:
An American organized crime group with origins in the Sicilian Mafia.

Lacerations:
Ragged wounds of body tissue, as from blows inflicted with a blunt instrument.

Lagnenomania:
Sadism in males.

Lands and grooves:
Raised and indented portions of a firearm barrel, generally known as rifling, that serve to impart a spin to the bullet. The cutting tools used in the rifling process often produce characteristic marks which may assist in individualized identification.

Larcenous intent:
The aim of depriving someone of his property.

Larceny by bailee:
Theft committed by a person responsible for guarding a particular piece of property who fraudulently transfers the ownership of that property to himself or to another person.

Larceny by fraud, deception, or trick:
Obtaining property from its owner by using fraudulent tactics.

Larceny from the person:
The theft of property from an individual without the use of violence.

Larceny, constructive:
Larceny in which felonious intent is inferred from the ac-

cuser's conduct even though the original taking of property did not appear felonious.

Larceny, simple:

Theft that does not entail violence in order to obtain the stolen property.

Larceny:

The crime of taking another's personal property without consent and with the felonies intent of depriving the owner of the property. This crime is often statutorily divide into different degrees, e.g., grand or petty larceny, with penalties differing. Degrees, e.g., grand or petty larceny, with penalties differing in severity.

The unlawful obtaining, taking, or withholding without force an item of value from another with the intent to permanently deprive; commonly known as theft.

Lascivious carriage:

Sexual acts, between members of the opposite sex, which are not punishable as crimes.

Lascivious cohabitation:

An offense committed by two unmarried individuals living together as a couple and engaging in sexual intercourse.

Lascivious:

Characterized by unrestrained and intense sexual feelings.

Latency:

The period of time that passes between the moment that a dosage of any drugs is administered and when the dosage to take effect.

Latent fingerprint:

A fingerprint accidentally left at the science of the crime but not visible unless treated in some way.

Latent fingerprints :

Ridge impressions located at a crime scene that are generally not visible before processing.

Latent heat of vaporization:

The amount of heat absorbed at the boiling point, under one atmosphere of pressure, when one gram of liquid changes into gas.

Latent heat:

The amount of heat necessary to move a solid substance beyond its melting point and convert it into a liquid, or the amount of hear necessary to move a liquid beyond its boiling, point and convert it into a gas. Scientific use.

Latent:

Potential, capable of being perceived with help e.g., latent fingerprint.

Lateral pressure:

Handwriting that contains visible horizontal movements of the pen due to a specific type of pressure by a writer.

Lathi:

A crowd control device constructed from a long stick with one end covered by a piece of metal.

Latin writing:

Written characters derived from the Roman alphabet and commonly used in both English and Western European alphabets.

Launder:

To invest illegally gained money in legitimate business enterprises.

Liberty:

The right of an individual to live in a society and to operate within the parameters of established rules and regulations, imposed in the interest of the community. At large, without fear or restraint from extraneous forces.

Libido:

Psychic energy, sexual urge, urge to obtain sensual satisfaction.

Lie detector:

Polygraph.

Lie:

To tell untruth in order to deliberately deceive.

Lineup:

An assembly of persons, including the suspect, viewed nor identification purposes by a crime victim or witness.

Liquid gold:

Amil nitrate. A drug used as a muscle relaxant to aid intercourse including anal intercourse.

Loan sharking:

The lending of money at exorbitant interest rates.

Loop fingerprint:

A fingerprint pattern characterized by ridges entering me side, recurring, and exiting the pattern, and also by the presence of type lines, delta, and core.

Loosening of associations:

Thinking characterized by speech in which ideas shift from one subject to other, that is completely unrelated or only obliquely related without speaker showing any awareness that the topics are unconnected.

Lunacy:

A mental disorder; Impaired faculties of the human mind; insanity.

Lust murder:

A homicide that often entails multination of sex organs.

Lust:

Insatiable desire for sexual activity.

Lymphadenopathy:

A condition of inflamed lymph glands in the body in areas other than groin.

Lynch law:

So- called justice out by the illegal execution of a person accused of crime and sentence to death by individuals with no legal right to try criminals cases.

Lynch mob:

A riotous and angry group of people that is bent upon killing, usually by illegally hanging someone whom they feel is guilty of a crime or whom they otherwise.

Lynch:

To execute by hanging without first providing the accused due process of law in traditional judicial arena.

Lysergic Acid Diethylamide (LSD):

An hallucinogenic originally derived from a rye fungus, first synthesized in 1938. Depending upon its chemical potency, the drug produces mild to psychotic-like hallucinations.

M

M1 rifle:
A clip-fed, semi-automatic 30-caliber rifle operating on gas; used by U.S. troops during WW-II.

Machlaenomania:
Masochism in females.

Mad:
Characterized by deficient mental abilities, craziness or insanity.

Madman:
An insane person. The term has no valid application either in the legal or medical profession.

Magpie:
A code word used by some paedophiles to identify each other. Believed to derive from magazine of the Pedophilia Information Exchange.

Make one's prints:
To identify a criminal from the fingerprints left behind at the scene of a crime.

Malice in fact:
The desire or intent to injure someone; either express or actual malice.

Malice in law:
Implied malice; presumed from acts committed without justification or excuse.

Malice:
The state of mind accompanying the intentional commission of a wrongful act without justification or excuse.

Malicious abuse of process:

The subversion of the judicial process to obtain an outcome that the law does not intend.

Malicious abandonment:

In criminal law, desertion of one's spouse without cause.

Malicious accusation:

An unjust charge based on a wrongful motive and lack or probable cause.

Malicious act:

An act committed with the intention to injure or damage without legal justification.

Malicious assault with a deadly weapon:

Aggravated assault using a gun, knife, or any other deadly weapon.

Malicious killing:

The intentional taking of someone's life without justification, and not within the sphere of voluntary manslaughter.

Malicious mischief:

Vandalism or defacement of another's personal property, carried out with malicious intent.

Malicious motive:

The desire to prosecute someone for reasons other than to brings him to justice.

Malicious prosecution:

A prosecution that has commence with the knowledge that the charges cannot be sustained. A legal action brought before a court by a person who has had criminal proceedings brought against him for malicious reasons and without probable cause.

Malicious trespass:

The deliberate destruction of private or public property.

Malicious:

Involving malice; regarding an act carried out wrongfully

and without justification.

Malinger:

To fake a sickness or injury for the express purpose of avoiding work or other responsibility.

Malingering:

Pretending to have a physical or mental disability or illness to postpone a trial or be assigned to less strenuous prison work.

Malpractice :

Careless or willful mistreatment of a medical patient by a medical doctor or public health official.

Man slayer:

One who kills a man.

Management by objective:

A management technique involving diagnosis of a problem, determination of proper action, evaluation of the action taken, and provision for necessary adjustments.

Mandamus:

A judicial writ issued to a corporation, its officer, or to an official or lower court, commanding a specific action or deed which is part of the person or entity's duty or responsibility; used only in extraordinary or emergency situations.

Mandatory sentence:

The minimum length of a prison sentence for various crimes, enacted into law by state legislatures.

Mandatory:

Required by law: obligatory; compulsory.

Manner of execution:

A legal requirement that law officers serve a search warrant in a carefully prescribed manner, e.g., the warrant must be executed at certain times of the day and to individuals of legal age.

Mannerism:

The repeated production of an action or utterance, less persistent than stereotype and more in keeping with personality characteristics.

Manslaughter:

The unlawful killing of a human without malice, generally specified as voluntary, involuntary, or reckless.

The unlawful killing of someone without malice, either express or implied. Voluntary or non- negligent manslaughter is the intentional killing of someone with provocations, as in the case of someone who is accidentally killed in a quarrel, the defendant was reasonably provoked to an act of violence, a charge of manslaughter rather than murder may be appropriate if the evidence suggests that some one else might have acted accordingly in similar circumstances, e.g., victims of adultery.

Manstealing:

Kidnapping or abduction.

Marauder:

One who searches for booty to steal.

Marijuana:

A dangerous drug produced by drying the leaves and flowering tops of the Cannabis plant.

Marijuana; mariguana; marhuana:

A depressant obtained from Cannabis sativa, the Indian hemp plant, an annual herb which grows wild in most tropical and temperate regions but cultivated throughout the world. The narcotic is derived from the parts of the plant that resin can be extracted from, including the leaves, flowers, and stem. Marijuana produces a relaxing euphoria and sometimes hallucinations. It is sometimes legally administered by physicians in some jurisdictions as a painkiller for patients undergoing chemotherapy or suffering from illnesses such as glaucoma. Additional to marijuana is more psychological than physical.

Masochism:

Sexual arousal from submission to pain or humiliation.

Submission to physical ill treatment at the hands of a sadist or another in order to achieve gratification, often of a sexual nature. Compare with *Sadism.*

Mastophallation:

Sexual activity by using the penis between a woman's breasts. A service increasingly offered by prostitutes since the advent of AIDS. A form of safe sex.

Masturbation:

Stimulation of the genitals to achieve pleasure.

Material witness:

A witness who possesses important information in reward to a criminal trial.

Mathemphetamine:

A dangerous drug that produces a stimulating effect on the central nervous system, which is more intense than simple amphetamine reactions.

Meapareunia:

Sexual act enjoyed by one partner only.

Measurement marker:

An easily recognizable object placed next to an item of evidence during crime-scene photography.

Meatus:

A hole or entrance to an organ such as is found in the tip of the penis.

Medical examiner:

A. physician, generally a forensic pathologist, who performs the duties traditionally entrusted to a coroner.

Melancholia:

A state of severe depression. It is considered a mental disease when the patient experiences periods of hallucination and is a danger to himself and others.

Melee:

A disorderly brawl, i.e. hand to-hand fighting among a

number of people.

Menage-a-trois:

Literally "a household of three", a situation where one married partner has a lover living with them with the consent of the other partner. Now used for any sexual activity involving three people.

Mens rea:

A guilty mind. The criminal state of mind or intent that accompanies a crime. The requisite state of mind varies depending upon the particular crime. The Model Penal code classifies crime into four different states of mind, or mens rea: crimes that require intention; crimes the require knowledge of the nature of the crime; crimes of recklessness that require that the person realize the degree of risk his actions entail; and crimes of gross negligence.

Mental alienation:

Insanity.

Mental capacity:

A person's psychological competence; one's understanding of the nature and consequences of an act about to be undertaken.

Mental cruelty:

Abusive behavior or conduct of one spouse towards another which makes a harmonious marriage all but impossible. The act of mental cruelty is normally grounds for divorce, but it is defined differently in various countries.

Mental deficiency:

A legal and scientific classification for individuals with arrested or incomplete social development. Once the mental deficiency has been established, the person will commonly fall into one of three categories: the idiot, with a mental and social age below three, the imbecile, or middle level, with a mental and social age between three and seven, and the moron, the highest grade, with a mental age between eight and twelve and a social age of between ten and twenty. These three classifications are frequently predicated on the results of I.Q. (intelligence quotient) and

S.Q. (social quotient) test.

Mental disease:

Diseased or defective condition of the mind. A lack of fitness to be held responsible for crime in a court of law.

Mental mechanisms:

The functions and variety of activity that go on inside the mind. Seventeen stages of activity have been identified by psychiatrists including identification. Sublimation, repression, reaction formation, undoing, isolation, displacement, symbolization, condensation, conversion, rationalization idealization, transference, projection, introjection, unconscious fantasy, and dreaming

Mental state:

The condition of a person's mind at the time a criminal act is committed.

Mental tests and measurements in criminology:

In analyzing a criminal offender's psychological state, various testing methods have been employed by social workers and criminologists over the years. The traditional approach as been to test for intelligence, using the Revised Stanford Binet Scale. Today, various psychological tests that include verbal and written sections are administered, making it possible to better gauge human behavior.

Meperidine:

The scientific Name of Demerol.

Mephentermine:

An over the counter amphetamine containing caffeine.

Meprobamate:

A mild sedative, but its continued used could result in dependency. Commonly known by its brand name Equanil.

Mescaline:

A hallucinogenic obtained from the peyote cactus that grows naturally in Mexico and the southwestern parts of the United States.

Methadone maintenance:

A treatment for heroin addiction involving the replacement of heroin with methadone,

Metropolitan Police Act:

English legislation that led to the development of the London Metropolitan Police.

Microcomputer:

A small computer system consisting of a keyboard and video screen.

Microphotography:

A class of photography in which the subject is enlarged.

Minge:

Slang, female pudendum- the expression dates from the turn of the century.

Misdemeanor:

An offense not as serious as a felony, generally punishable by incarceration in a correctional facility for up to, but not more than, a year.

Modus operandi:

The specific method of operation employed by a criminal during the commission of an offense which is likely to be repeated to form an identifiable pattern.

Molotov coktail:

A homemade firebomb, made with an empty bottle, some flammable liquid and a wick inserted into the neck. The device is named after V.M. Molotov, A Russian statesmen.

Mood:

A pervasive and sustained state of feeling which in extreme or morbid degree can dominate the subject's internal and exernal outlook.

Mooning:

Indecent exposure of the buttocks.

Morphine:

The principal alkaloid of opium converted through a boiling and filtering process.

MOTAS:

Intrnet acronym for "member of the appropriate sex".

MOTOS:

Internet acronym for "member of the opposite sex",

MOTSS:

Internet acronym for "member of the same sex".

Muff-diving:

Oral sex on a woman.

Multiagency Unit:

Two or more law enforcement agencies working jointly to apply combined resources to one or more criminal investigations.

Murder:

The unlawful killing of a human with malice aforethought.

Mutism:

Refusal to speak for conscious or unconscious reasons.

N

Narcoanalysis:

A medical interviewing technique in which drug compounds are used.

Narcolepsy:

A paroxysmal disorder, characterized by sudden irresistible tendency to fall asleep, usually for short period.

Narcosis:

A feeling or state of unconsciousness or suspended animation produced by use of narcotics or similar chemicals.

Narcotest:

An examination to discover if a person is or was using drugs.

Narcotic addict:

A Person who has a physical and psychological dependency on narcotic drugs.

Narcotic antagonist:

A drug designed to counteract the effects of an overdose of narcotics.

Narcotic drugs:

Drugs regulated by federal and state laws, which are classified in the followings five groups marijuana, opium and derivatives, coca plant substances, the meperdine group, and any synthetically derived drugs.

Narcotic tolerance:

Physical need for increasing narcotic quantities to achieve the initial effect of the substance.

Narcotic:

A drug that dulls the sense, alleviates pain, and induces sleep, e.g, morphine, heroin, opium, marijuana, or LSD

In a medical sense, it refers to opium and opium derivatives or synthetic substitutes; in a legal sense, other non-opium substances are included.

Narcotics paraphernalia:

Items used in connection with injecting, ingesting, or smoking various narcotics and dangerous drugs.

National Crime Information Center:

A computerized center operated by the FBI to assist law enforcement agencies in the apprehension of suspects and recovery of stolen property.

Necrophilia:

Intercourse with a dead body.

Necrophilism:

A form of insanity in which one desires to be near or touch dead bodies, especially in a sexual manner.

Negativism:

Verbal or non verbal opposition or resistance to outside suggestions and advice.

Negligence, criminal:

Negligence involving a greater deviation from the levels of care required for civil liability, justifying the imposition of criminal sanctions. Must be a greater degree of unreasonableness than is involved in negligence, e.g., reckless disregard for the safety of others.

Negligence, gross:

Willful disregard for one's actions and the resulting consequences.

Negligence:

Failure to exercised the degree of care which a reasonable person, i.e., one of ordinary prudence would exercise in similar circumstances.

Negligent homicide:

A criminal offense by one whose negligence causes another's death, i.e., involving the negligent operation of a motor vehicle.

Negligent manslaughter:

A death that results from neglect of ordinary precaution without malicious intent often a statutory crime,.

Negotiated plea:

Plea bargaining in which the defendant agrees to plead guilty in exchange for the prosecutor's recommendation for a reduced sentence.

Neighborhood:

A systematic checking of residences near a crime scene for investigative leads.

Nembutal:

A sleep-producing barbiturate used for fast-acting sedation. It is a trade name of pentobarbital.

Neologism:

New words invented by an individual, distortions of words or standard words to which the individual assigns a new and highly idiosyncratic meaning.

Neuroleptic:

A sleep-inducing drung designed to reduce uneasiness and mental strain.

Neurosis:

A behavior disorder without apparent physical cause.

Neurotic disorder, Neuroses:

A mental disorder without any demonstrable organic basis in which the patient may have considerable insight and has unimpaired reality testing. Behaviour may be greatly affected although usually remaining within socially acceptable limits. Personality is not disorganized. The principal manifestations include excessive anxiety, hysterical symptoms, phobias, obsessive and compulsive symptoms, and depression.

Neutralize:

To nullify the effects or activities of something.

Neutron activation analysis (NAA):

A nuclear method of determining the presence and composition of trace elements by bombarding a substance with neutron particles.

Neutron-activation analysis:

A scientific that shows the contents of certain materials, esp. weaponry.

Nolo contendere:

A judicial plea declaring that the defendant will not contest the charge(s), but will not admit formal guilt.

Nondiscernible microbionoculator:

A poisoned dart gun that is concealed.

Not guilty by reason of insanity:

A verdict that the accused in innocent of the charges by virtue of being insane when the crime was committed, usually The jury is asked to determine whether the defendant is guilty or no, before deciding the question of insanity.

Not guilty plea:

A formal answer by the defendant stating that he is innocent of the charges brought against him.

Not guilty:

A decision by the judge or jury that the accused is return a guilty verdict.

Notorious cohabitation:

The statutory offense of two persons living together without being married.

Nymphomania:

An ungovernable desire to have sex. Used only in regard to women; a similar condition in men is called satyriasis.

O

Oath purgatory:

A statement made by someone in an effort to clear himself of suspicious, charges, or contempt of court.

Oath:

A declaration of the truth or that one will tell the truth.

Objection:

Opposition to a procedure or evidence put forth by the other party during a trial. An objection made during open court will be useful if an appeal is to be made.

Obliterate:

To kill or completely and utterly destroy.

Obscene telephone call:

A phone call in which the called uses sexual language, usually to someone unknown to the general populace.

Obscene:

That which does not meet acceptable standards of decency. In regard to sexual behavior, something is obscene if the average person views it as fulfilling a purely prurient interest.

Observation:

The watching of an object that does not move, e.g., building.

Obsession:

A persistent unwanted idea, impulse, image or doubt that cannot be eliminated by logic or reasoning. These are invariably distressing, and the individual often tries, though unsuccessfully to resist them. They are, however, recognized as the individual's own thoughts, even though they are involuntary and often repugnant.

Obstructing justice:

Inhabiting the way of lawful proceeding or hindering justice in any way e.g., getting in the way of police investigation, preventing subpoenas from being served or witnesses from testifying.

Obstructing an officer:

Forcibly resisting a police officer from carrying out his duties.

Obstructing process:

Purposefully preventing or attempting to prevent a legal process from taking place.

Obstruction:

Someone or something that prevents an act from being carried out, e.g., an obstruction of justice.

Obtain:

To come into possession of property or money.

Occasional criminal:

One who commits a crime to fulfill an immediate want or need rather than as a way of life.

Oedipus complex:

An emotional condition in which the person has unconscious, intense affections, usually sexual, for one's parent of the opposite sex, with strong feeling against the other parent.

Offense:

An act that breaks the law, usually a misdemeanor or felony violating public and private rights.

Offensive weapon:

An instrument used primarily for attacking someone with injuries intent, e.g., dangerous weapon.

Omission:

Failure to act as the law require or commission of crime by neglecting one's duties.

Onanism:

Self-masturbation.

Once in jeopardy:

The circumstance in which the accused has faced lawful proceedings once before for the same crime.

Open prison:

A prison that does not have locks on doors or bars on windows.

Operation Identification:

A system of identifying valuable in the home, as a deterrent to crime, since items the owners can positively, identify are more likely to be returned.

Opiate:

A drug produced from the juice of unripe seed pods of the opium plant, e.g., heroin or morphine, or those synthetically produced but having similar qualities.

Opium:

A narcotic substance extruded from a type of poppy plant. Frequently used illegally but also used legally in medicine.

An addictive narcotic taken from the seeds of an oriental poppy (Papaver somniferum), which can be used as a pain reliever. The drug has gummy, tar-like texture and is dark brown in appearance. The non- medicinal opium, which is smoked, is produced by adding raw opium to water and boiling it.

Opponent:

A person who oppose another.

Oppression:

Abuse of authority by a person in power.

Opprobrium:

Public disgrace brought about by wrongly action or grossly vicious conduct.

Oppugn:

To attack another

Oral confession:

An admission of guilt by the defendant that may not be admissible in court. Generally the prosecution must prove the confession's admissibility by showing that it was given voluntarily, legal procedures were followed, and other factors.

Orange:

An amphetamine, especially a Dexedrine pill that is colored orange and heart-shaped.

Ordinance:

A law of a state subdivision, such as a county, city, or village.

A statute, rule, or regulation enforced by a political unit smaller than a state, e.g., a country or city, where fines are imposed for disobedience.

Ordinance:

Military weaponry, e.g., the weapons themselves, ammunition, and the vehicles that carry heavy guns.

Organized crime:

Pertaining to the criminal activities of any group of individuals who have formed a highly organized, disciplined association engaged primarily in illegal operations.

Outfit:

Narcotics paraphernalia used to inject a substance into the bloodstream; also known as an injection kit.

Outline note-taking:

Crime scene or field notes that are arranged in traditional outline form, generally by time sequence or some other orderly fashion.

P

Paederasty (pederasty):

Anal sex with a young boy.

Paedophilia:

Love for young children.

Paid informant:

An individual who receives monetary compensation for providing information to a law enforcement agency.

Pander:

A pimp.

Panic attacks:

Discrete periods of sudden onset of intense apprehension, fearfulness or terror, often associated with feelings of impending doom and sympathetic overactivity.

Paraffin test:

A method of determining whether or not a suspect as fired a firearm within a given time period by coating the hands with melted paraffin to note the presence of or absence of nitrates. This method of testing is often replaced by the more reliable neutron activation analysis method.

Paraldehyde:

A liquid nonbarbiturate hypnotic that acts upon the central nervous system as a depressant, has effects similar to barbiturates, and can be used to treat delirium tremens.

Paramour:

A lover, especially an illicit lover.

Once who assists a lawyer, by performing such tasks as assembling documents and summarizing depositions.

Paranoia:

A mental disease in which the patient functions normally,

except that he erroneously thinks that he is being persecuted or wronged.

A mental disorder charactrized by fixed delusions, typically of a suspicious nature.

Paranoid:

A descriptive term designating either morbid dominant ideas or delusions of self reference concerning one or more of several themes; most commonly persecution, love, hate, envy, jealousy, honour, litigation, supernatural and grandeur.

Paraph:

An extra stroke at the end of a signature. Handwriting analysis use.

Paraphernalia:

Accessory equipment or items, often refers to equipment used in taking drugs.

Pardon:

An action by a governing power such as a governor or the President that frees one from the punishment normally administered for a crime.

Paregoric:

A mild narcotic and medicine that contains traces of opium extract, frequently used for diarrhoea and sometimes abused by drug addicts. The scientific name is camphorated opium tincture.

Parents Anonymous :

A support group for parents to help prevent child abuse, juvenile alcoholism, delinquency, and drug addiction.

Paresis:

Gradual paralysis, usually caused by syphilis, and often leading to a form of insanity; Dementia Paralytica- a condition sometimes called softening of the brain.

Parliamentary:

An early English practice in which officials were paid for

the apprehension and prosecution of criminals, thus encouraging a high arrest and conviction rate.

Parole:

A conditional and revocable early release from a correctional institution.

Partial fingerprint:

A latent fingerprint in which only a portion of the pattern area is visible or able to be recovered.

Passivity feelings:

Morbid experiences in clear consciousness, in which thoughts, emotions, reactions, or bodily activities appear to be influenced/ "made", directed or controlled by an external agency or force, human or inhuman.

PBZ:

The antihistamine pyribenzamine, which is combined with other drugs to enhance their effects.

PCP:

Phencyclidine, a dangerous hallucinogen. The drug can cause numbness, sensory distortion, paranoia, and psychoses that are indistinguishable from schizophrenia. In pure form, PCP is white crystalline powder which, when mixed other ingredients, turns tan or brown. The drug is sold in powder, liquid, tablet, or capsule form. The drug is taken by smoking, snorting, or injecting and has been linked to murder, suicide, and accidental death.

Pedophilia:

The sexual desire of an adult to fondle or sexually violate a child.

Peeping Tom:

Voyeur

Perjury:

The intentional making of a false statement while under oath to tell the truth during a judicial proceeding.

Perplexity:

A state of puzzled bewilderment in which verbal responses are desultary and disjointed, reminiscent of confusion.

Perseveration:

Repetition of an action or utterance which has just been carried out when the patient desires or is requested to initiate (which is purposeless, though was relevant carlier)

Petty theft:

A legal distinction of larceny in which the value of the stolen object results in a misdemeanor prosecution.

Phencyclidine:

A powerful synthetic hallucinogenic compound originally developed as an anesthetic.

Phenobarbital:

A barbiturate, also called purple hearts.

Phentermine:

A appetite suppressant drug. Ionamin and Adipex- P are two popular types.

Pherenology:

A concept widely accepted from 1850- 1900 that was used to analyze one's psychological characteristics, including any criminal tendencies, based on the theory that the mind could be divided into faculties and functions, which were related to the skull's shape. Pioneered by Alphonse Bertillon.

Philadelphia lawyer:

A clever lawyer adroit at utilizing legal technicalities to his favor.

Phobia:

Irrational fear of an object, place, person or situation accompanied by avoidance behaviour.

Phone freak:

One who can get by without paying at a pay phone.

Phonoscopy:

Study, analysis, and identification of voiceprints.

Photo surveillance:

Recording the movements of suspects by cameras.

Photography:

Photography has become an important tool for police investigations. Photographs are taken of crime scenes to show the relationship of something being investigated to other fixed objects in the area. Infrared or ultraviolet photos can be used to detect forgeries. Sometime photograph are enlarged to try to glean information not otherwise noticeable. Pictures are also taken of prisoners for identification.

Physical dependence:

An acquired need of the body to continue receiving some substance to continue functioning as it has been. The body adjusts to drug levels, and when drug presence drops to a certain level, sometimes begins to require the drug. At this point, if the body does not continue to get the drug, the user begins to experience withdrawal symptoms. Withdrawal symptoms vary according to the type of drug and the amount used by the addict.

Physical description:

A description of someone's physical features.

Physical evidence:

Evidence of a tangible nature which may be of importance during an investigation or a subsequent judicial proceeding.

Physiognomy:

The discernment of criminal characteristics from facial features.

Physiological dependence:

An addiction to drugs.

Pigeon drop swindle:

A common bunco method of operation in which a victim is persuaded to produce money in order to share in the division of "found" money. By sleight of hand, or some other technique, the victim's "good faith" money is stolen.

Pimp:

One who obtains clients for a prostitute.

Pistol:

A handgun that operates on a blow-back principle: the force of the discharge ejects the fired casing, loading and cocking the weapon for the next firing.

Plate:

Oral sex.

Plea bargaining:

A legal practice involving an agreement between the prosecutor and the defense counsel in which a plea of guilty is accepted in exchange for a reduction of charges.

Point of ignition :

The specific location within an arson crime scene where the fire was started.

Poker:

A card game, with several possible variations, involving betting by players as to who holds the hand of highest value. A player bets that his hand will beat the hands of all other participants. The other players are required to match the bet placed, raise, the stakes, or drop out of the game. end is the winner.

Police brutality:

The practice by some law enforcement officers of employing excessive force during the arrest of criminal suspects.

Police corruption:

Dishonest use of police power for profit or favours.

Police court:

In some countries, a lesser court that has authority over minor infractions, traffic and city ordinance violations, some matters of the justice of the peace, and certain civil cases; may conduct preliminary hearings for those accused of more serious crimes.

Police criminalistics:

The process used to gather facts in crime detection.

Police department:

A government department of law enforcement officials whose responsibility is to keep public order and safety and to prevent and detect criminal offenders.

Police dog:

A dog, often a German shepherd, trained to protect people or property, to sniff out smuggled items, tack criminals, or control mobs.

Police force:

A group of trained police officials who are responsible for keeping the public peace and safety and preventing and discovering crime.

Policedom:

A Police system.

Policeman:

A male police officer.

Polygraph:

An instrument that measures certain physiological changes of the body, triggered by emotional responses to specific verbal questions; generally used to determine deception.

Ponce:

(1) one who lives off the earnings of a prostitute; (2) a homosexual.

Pornography:

Subject matter that is judged to be morally offensive to the degree of being obscene. There is considerable latitude over what constitutes pornographic or obscenity.

Portrait parle:

A dark blue discoloration of parts of the body nearest the ground; an after death process due to the force of gravity. Color may also be cherry red or pink depending upon the cause of death.

Posturing:

Strange, fixed and bizzare bodily positions held by a patient for a long time.

Precipitin test:

A laboratory test to determine whether a blood sample is of animal or human origin.

Predatory criminal:

A criminal type characterized by crimes which involve confrontation and the selection or stalking of vulnerable victims.

Preliminary hearing:

A judicial examination of the arrest and charges brought against the accused.

Preliminary investigation:

The first exposure of a criminal offense to the investigative process.

Preliminary report:

The first formal reporting of a criminal of Tense, used as the foundation report for all subsequent reports.

Premeditation:

A degree of planning and forethought sufficient to indicate the intention to commit a crime.

Pressure of speech:

Rapid, accelerated, frenzied speech, which sometimes exceeds the ability of the vocal musculature to articulate, leading to jumbled and cluttered speech. At other times, it exceeds the ability of the listener to comprehend, as the speech expresses a flight of ideas or an unintelligible jargon.

Prince Albert:

Male genital piercing. It is said that Prince Albert had a penile ring designed to hold back his foreskin. The term is used for all male genital piercing but is often used to describe a mental bar totally transfixing the scrotum.

Priority assignment:

A case assignment method in which investigations are assigned by their perceived importance.

Prison labor:

Work done by convicts, including building and repairing roads, manufacturing license plates, and making furniture for public schools.

Prison psychosis:

A mental disorder in which one, esp. a criminal, has a fear of imprisonment.

Prison reform:

Plants to change prisons to encourage rehabilitation. Imprisonment instead of corporeal punishment, the workhouse, separation of mentally ill from criminals, job assistance, and probation were all introduced by prison-reform movements.

Prison sentence:

A penalty for which a criminal is sent to a correctional facility for confinement.

Prison van:

A van used to carry arrested people to jail or prisoners to and from court.

Prison visiting:

Period of time during which visitors, including friends, relatives, lawyers, and clergy can visit prisoners. The length of the visits varies from fifteen minutes to more than an hour. Visitors are searched to prevent them from smuggling items to prisoners.

Prison within a prison:

A cell for solitary confinement.

Privacy, right of:

The right of an individual to be left to himself, without unnecessary publicity and without unjustified government interference in his relationships, his family, or his activities.

Private detective:

One who investigates a matter for a group or individual other than on behalf of the public. Private detective are usually licensed by state.

Private eye:

A private detective

Private Investigator:

Nonsworn investigators who are paid by private citizens and organizations to gather information id private matters, generally of a civil rather than criminal nature. A small percentage of private agency cases may be concerned with criminal defense.

Privilege against self-incrimination:

The right guarantee by the Constitution not to testify against oneself that a defendant may invoke if he is called to the witness stand against his wished, but that is waives if he voluntarily takes the stand.

Privilege from arrest:

A privilege, temporary or permanent, that is granted to people such as foreign ministers or witnesses, exempting them from prosecution for some criminal charges.

Privileged communications:

Information obtained in certain confidential relationships that would not ordinarily be received in evidence.

Privileged evidence:

Protected information that generally does not have to be divulged, such as classified government information, an informant's name, some kinds of accident reports or the proceedings of a grand jury.

Privileged relationship:

The special relationship such as between husband and wife or lawyer and client, which the law sometimes protects by forbidding the forcing of one to take the stand to reveal communications from the other.

Proactive policing:

Law enforcement efforts which respond to a crime threat before the commission of the offense rather than reacting to a victimization.

Probable cause hearing:

A procedure in a criminal case in which a judge determines whether a complaint should be issued or the case sent to a grand jury.

Probable cause:

In a criminal case, reasonable grounds to believe that a person should be arrested or searched, or that property subject to search and seizure is at a certain.

Reasonable grounds to connect a suspect to a crime and justifying various searches and/or an arrest.

Probation:

A sentence allowing a convicted person to avoid confinement with the stipulation that he be supervised by a probation officer and that he maintain good conduct. If he violates the terms of his probation, he can be brought before, a court.

A conditional sentence that avoids imprisonment if the offender agrees to and abides by the requirements of the court.

Progress report:

An investigative report regarding a specific criminal investigation that formally documents the progress, or lack of, investigative leads.

Prosecutor:

A lawyer who acts on behalf of the government during a criminal proceeding.

Provost court:

A military court hearing minor criminal cases in unfriendly occupied territory

Provost guard:

A group of soldiers acting as police for the provost marshal.

Proxenetism:

Pimping by other women.

Prurient:

Characterized by lewdness or lasciviousness.

Pseudodementia:

A syndrome, in which dementia is mimicked by functional psychiatric illness. Symptoms are similar to those found in case of dementia. Depression in elderely may present as dementia.

Pseudolalia fantastica:

A condition in which one accuses oneself of a crime not committed.

Pseudonym:

An alias.

Psilocybe:

Hallucinogenic fungi or mushrooms used by some tribes of American and Mexican Indians. The mushrooms contain psilocybin and psilocyn.

Psilocybin:

A natural hallucinogenic compound obtained from mushrooms.

Psychedelia:

Environment with mind altering drugs, drug, users, and drug paraphernalia.

Psychedelic drugs:

Drugs, including LSD, mescaline, and psilocybin.

Psychedelic experiences:

Distortions of touch, vision, sound emotional reactions, and hallucinations.

Psychedelicatessen:

A shop that sells drug paraphernalia.

Psychiatry:

A branch of medicine concerned with mental disorder, including its study, diagnosis, prevention, and treatment.

Psychic dependence:

Continued used of drugs to obtain a "normal state"

Psychical:

Of the mind or soul.

Psycho ward:

A hospital ward for psychopaths.

Psycho:

A psychotic personality.

Psychoanalysis:

The method of treating psychotic behavior and other emotional or mental disorders developed by Sigmund Freud. Freud believed that all behavior was a result of the forces acting upon the unconscious part of the human brain, and that personality disorder could be cured by exploring the unconscious through free association, interpretation of dreams, and resistance and transfer analysis.

Psycho-diagnosis:

An examination of a patent's mental condition, determined by the result of psychological test and past history.

Psychogenic:

A term used widely and loosely to indicate attribution of aetiology or pathogenesis to mental, psychological or emotional factors rather than a physical cause.

Psychological profiling:

An attempt to identify crime perpetrators through the application of psychological theory, crime-scene review, and victim/witness statement analysis.

Psychology:

The science concerned with ways to gauge, understand, the alter mental activities and behavior. The emotional, mental and behavioral traits of an individual.

Psychomotor excitement:

Generalized physical and emotional overactivity in response to internal and external stimuli. Seen in schizophrenia and mania.

Psychomotor retardation:

A generalized slowing of physical and emotinal reactions. Seen in depression and schizophrenia.

Psychoneurosis:

A behavioral or emotional disorder with no physical source or change, including mania, mania hallucinatoria, primary acute dementia, and melancholia.

Psychopath:

A mentally ill or unstable individual who is typically incapable of normal feelings of guilt. Also known as sociopath, such people are also characterized by their need for immediate gratification and their ability to manipulate others.

One who suffers from a mental disorder in which he perceives reality, but does not understand social or moral responsibility and commits crimes or is involved in bizarre behavior of instant gratification. The psychopath completely disregards the welfare of other and is unable to establish meaningful relationship with others.

Psychopathic personality:

Criminal character, a criminal psychopath.

Psychopathology:

The study of the psychological and social impact of drugs.

Psychopharmacology:

The study of mental abnormalities.

Psychoquack:

An unqualified, uncertified psychiatrist or psychologist.

Psychosis:

A mental disorder in which an individual has difficulty sustaining relationships, shows no concern for social convention, has time and space distortions, experience breaks with reality, and has extreme departures from normal through and actions; more sever than a psychoneurosis.

Psychotherapy:

A form of psychological treatment in which a trained person establishes a professional contract with the patient and through definite therapeutic communications, both verbal and non-verbal, attempts to alleviate the emotional disturbances, reverse or change maladaptive patterns of behaviour and encourages personality growth and development.

A treatment for nervous disorders, especially by conversation between patient and doctor, the doctor encourages and motivates the patient, and sometimes prescribes drugs.

Psychotic disorder, psychosis:

Mental disorder in which a person's thoughts, affective responses, ability to recognize reality, and ability to relate to and communicate with others are sufficiently impaired to interfere with his capacity to deal with reality. Classical features are delusions, hallucinations and impaired reality testing.

Psychotic personality:

An individual who cannot function normally; he usually cannot reason well, has great mental and emotional swings, and may be dangerous to himself and others.

Psychotic:

An individual suffering from a severe mental illness characterized by the inability to determine reality.

Psychotomimetics:

Drug that case temporary psychotic like symptoms in the user.

Psychotoxic:

Of a drug, capable of changing behavior by altering his mood.

Psychotropics:

Drugs, such as hashish, marijuana, antidepressants, hallucinogens, and tranquilizers, that affect mood and behavior, but do not depress the central nervous system.

Psycho-weaponry:

Psychological intimidation used by terrorists, such as threatening to kill or injure their victims.

Puberty:

The point of physical development at which an individual can begin to reproduce.

Public defender:

A lawyer who represents indigent defendants who cannot afford a lawyer's services. The lawyer generally either works for the government or is a private attorney appointed by the court.

Public investigators:

Sworn or nonsworn investigators employed by a public agency who perform specific information-gathering tasks.

Public nuisance:

One who does something to harm a community. An action or a neglected action that harm the community or a significant number of person; e.g., a condition endangering public health.

Public offense:

An act or omission prohibited and punishable by law; characterizes crimes as opposed to civil infringements on private rights.

Public prosecutor:

An attorney working for the government whose job is to prosecute accused criminals.

Public prosecutor:

An attorney working for the government whose jobs is to prosecute accused criminals.

Public servant:

An official or employee of the government.

Public trial:

A trail that is open to the general public.

Pudendum:

External genitals especially of a woman. Literally means: "the parts one should be ashamed of".

Puerperal insanity:

A mental disorder in women during or just after the time when they give birth to a child, also called "eclampsia parturientium".

Punch attack:

A method of safe burglary in which the dial is removed by force leaving the spindle and locking mechanism open to attack.

Pussy or Puss:

The female vulva "to eat pussy" – to perform cunnilingus.

Putrefaction:

Postmortem darkening of the skin accompanied by bloating due to bacterial gases.

Pyromaniac:

An individual who sets fires due to a compulsive mental illness.

Q

Quackery:

The practice or art to pretending to posses medical knowledge and skill.

Quacksalver:

A medical quack.

Quail:

A young child, a girl under the age of consent (used by paedophiles).

Quarantine:

Required isolation of people, animals, areas, plants, or containers that are suspected carriers of a communicable disease.

Quarry:

A person being chased or pursued.

Quasi judicial:

Characterized by a partly judicial nature, in that hearing and investigation of a particular matter are performed similarly to judicial review but without the power or authority of the judiciary.

Queer:

Homosexual (usually applied to male homosexuals). The term was originally intended as an insult but has recently become acceptable to some homosexuals.

Quinine:

A drug used to cut heroin, because its bitter taste is similar to heroin's

R

R.A.D.:
Reflex anal dilation- a possible sign of anal abuse.

Rack:
1.a. device that stretches the body for purposes of torture.

Racket:
Any criminal act, operation, or career, so- called because of the disturbance it creates. Most rackets reap fast profits by fooling many people at once, e.g., through illicit sporting events that are tied to gambling operations.

Racketeer:
A criminal or unethical person. An extortionist.

Rackets:
Extremely competitive, large, ongoing criminal operations. The first successful racketeers were reasonably respected and admired by the public, who built up these criminal's business by spending money on their illegal games and drugs.

Radar speedalyzer:
An automatic radar controlled device used by the police to determine the traveling speed of motor vehicles.

Radial fracture lines:
Glass fractures which result from the bending of the pane towards a striking force causing jagged lines from the point of impact outward. The lines are more common on the side of the glass opposite the striking force.

Radio codes:
The numerical system used by police officers in radio communications.

Rape trauma syndrome:
A common rape victimization reaction characterized by emo-

tional distress, denial, delay of reporting, anger, guilt, or unusual calm after the attack.

Rape without force or consent:

Sexual intercourse with a person of legal age of consent, but who is unconscious or whose judgment or self- control are impaired by mental defects or intoxicants such as drugs or alcohol.

Rape, forcible:

Criminal sexual intercourse with another by violence or threats of violence.

Rape, sodomite:

Anal intercourse with a man or woman by violence or threat of grave injury.

Rape:

Forcible sexual intercourse with a person without his or her consent.

The act of sexual intercourse by force, or against the victims will.

Rapee:

A rape victim.

Rapist:

One who rapes.

Reality testing:

The ability to evaluate the external world objectively and to differentiate adequately between it and the internal world.

Recidivist:

A repeat offender who commits additional crimes after having been arrested or imprisoned for criminal activity in the past.

Rectangular coordinate:

A crime-scene sketching method in which two right angles are drawn from the evidence item to the nearest permanent object.

Regulate:

To control or govern according to prescribed law.

Regulation:

An order or rule that carries the force of a law issued by the executive of government.

Rehabilitate:

To reform; to return to society.

Rehabilitation:

The reformation of a criminals so that he may return to society.

Release procedures:

Methods of releasing prisoners, which are divided into two categories; unconditional and conditional release. Unconditional release includes pardon, expiration of sentence, and commutation of sentence. Conditional release includes conditional pardon and parole. Probation is not included because it is initiated by court order and is not an administrative act.

Relevant evidence:

Evidence that helps to prove or disprove matters at issues

Remand:

The sending of a prisoner back to court to attend or continue a hearing. The sending of a prisoner back to confinement.

Remission:

A state of partial or complete reduction or abatement of the symptoms and signs of a disorder.

Rent-boy:

Male prostitute, a catamite.

Renunciation:

A lawbreaker's denouncement of and withdrawal from criminal behavior.

Reparation:

Satisfaction given or amends made for a wrong committed.

Repeal:

To revoke or void an existing law by an official action especially enactment of a new law.

Repeat offenders:

Criminals who are convicted more than once, esp. for the same offense. More common for felons than for those convicted of misdemeanors, according to recent studies.

Repleader:

The right to plead a case a second time because of a miscarriage of justice.

Represent:

To act on behalf of or for another in a legal proceeding.

Repressive terrorism:

Any criminal act designed to eliminate informants, rivals, or any person failing to conform to the demands of the terrorists.

Reprieve:

A temporary postponement of a criminal sentence or punishment, usually granted to a prisoner so that he can attempt to obtain a lighter sentence.

Reprimand:

A formal or severe rebuke. To rebuke harshly or formally.

Reprisal:

A retaliatory act.

Reprove:

To convict.

Repudiate:

To reject or refuse to acknowledge

Res gestae:

Spontaneous words or phrases spoken during the commission of an offense; generally admissible evidence during a judicial proceeding.

Resin:

The sticky substance found in marijuana or hashish, which yields tetrahydrocannabinol, THC, the active ingredient found in those drugs.

Resist:

To oppose by exertion of force, e.g., resist arrest.

Resisting an officer:

The criminal deterrence of an officer from the commission of his duties, usually to avoid arrest.

Respite:

A temporary postponement, e.g., a stay of execution.

Response time:

The time required for law enforcement officers to arrive at a crime scene after receiving a complaint or call for service.

Restitution:

A statutory programs under which a lawbreaker must repay the victim or society with money or services as part of his punishment. Many juvenile criminals are paroled if they return stolen goods to their rightful owner or perform community work. The return of stolen items or other valuable goods that were unlawfully obtained.

Retifism:

Foot fetish.

Revolver:

A handgun in which a revolving multichambered cylinder aligns with the barrel prior to discharge.

Reward program:

Programs operated by law enforcement or citizen groups which encourage the reporting of criminal activities or investigative information.

Rigor mortis:

A postmortem stifferning of the muscles in the jaw and neck area and spreading downward through the body.

Rim service:

Anal sex.

Rim:

Anus

Rip attack:

A method of safe burglary in which the exterior metal sheets of the safe are peeled from a weakened corner location.

Robbery:

The taking of property from a person, or immediate presence of that person, by the use of force or by threat of the imminent use of force.

Rubber:

U.S. slang-condom.

Rule of discovery:

The pretrial right of the adversary to examine documents, reports, and other types of information in the possession of the opposition that are anticipated to be introduced as evidence during the trial; created primarily for the benefit of the defendant.

S

S&M:

Sado-masochism.

Sabotage:

The deliberate destruction of property belonging to a government, its military installations (political sabotages), an agency, or a private company (industrial sabotage), intended to severely crippled their resources and output.

Saboteur:

An individual who commits an act of sabotage.

Sacrilege:

Violation of the sacred tenets of the church. This usually involves a vandalism of church or synagogue property, theft, or malicious mischief carried out with evil intent.

Sadism:

Sexual arousal from inflicting pain or humiliation or by domination.

The infliction of pain on living thing as a mean of obtaining pleasure, typically of a sexual nature.

Sado-masochism:

A condition in which one is gratified sexually by both administering and receiving pain.

Sadomasochist:

A sexual deviant who enjoys receiving pain and inflicting physical and emotional torment on his or her partner.

Sanity hearing:

A judicial procedure or examination ordered by the court to determine whether a defendant is legally sane.

Saphism:

Love or sex between women.

School forms:

The method of teaching handwriting in school.

Scienter (Lat):

Literally meaning, knowingly; in criminal law, the defendant's previous knowledge of an illegal act.

Scientific Investigation:

A division of the police department involved in the analysis of criminal evidence, or items relating to the commission of a crime.

Scoundrel:

A person lacking moral precepts, dignity, and principle.

Sealing of records:

A policy in some jurisdictions which safeguards a defendant's privacy by having all his criminal records removed from the public domain. Persons seeking to examine a document would have to secure approval from the court or a designated official. This is usually done in cases involving underage offenders.

Search incident to arrest:

The discretionary power granted to the police by the courts to search a suspect or the immediate area around him at the time of arrest. The police generally may search the suspect's person or areas within his immediate control, i.e. areas into which he might reach to grab a weapon or destroy evidence. If police want to search any other area at or after the time of arrest, a search warrant generally must be obtained.

Search warrant:

A written court order authorizing the police to search a specific premise for stolen property or illegal substances and to seize and produce the property before the court.

An order issued by a judge authorizing a policemen or special agent to search for and seize an individual or certain property, from a private residence, place of business, or other location.

Search:

A thorough investigation made of a person, his property or

other possessions, to establish guilt or to determine if he has concealed some illegal contraband, or items that would relate to a specific criminal action for which he is charged. This would refer to any police or government search conducted without a properly executed warrant.

Second-degree crime:
Less serious by its very nature, second degree crime carries with it weaker penalties. Some local jurisdictions define various criminal acts in first, second, and third degrees. The punishment is commensurate with the act.

Second-degree murder:
Generally defined as the taking of a person's life with malice aforethought but without the premeditation or deliberation found in first-degree murder.

Sector search:
A crime scene searching technique in which the area to be searched is divided into equal areas of searching responsibility.

Security and privacy standards:
The steps that are taken to ensure that the records of criminal and juvenile offenders are kept confidential.

Security guard:
One who provides security for a location or people.

Security:
The measures employed to guard a military, government, or corporate installation from acts of espionage, sabotage, and infiltration. 2. The varying degrees or prisoner incarceration necessary to safeguard the institution, and the other inmates, e.g., minimum and maximum security, solitary confinement of an individual, etc.

Sedative:
Any drug that tranquilizes or induces the user to sleep.,

Seditions:
Advocating sedition.

Seditious libel:
Any book, pamphlet, or article written no incite others to overthrow of the government by force or to change the government through unlawful means.

Seditious speech:
Spoken words that encourage or advocate the violent overthrow of the government.

Seduce:
To coax, persuade, or otherwise entice another into an act of fornication or adultery through promises, kind words, or bribery. To entice someone to perform a criminals act: to corrupt

Seduction:
The act of compelling someone without force to sacrifice chastity, or to be compromised in a sexual manner.

Segregation:
Policy of incarcerating criminals in order to keep them away the rest of society. The confinement of a problem prisoner to a solitary cell.

Seizure:
The act of taking a person or his property into custody.

Self- murder:
Suicide.

Self-incrimination:
Characteristic of involving oneself with a crime.

Self-loading:
Relating to a semi-automatic gum.

Self-slaughter:
Suicide.

Self-slaughtered:
Murdered by oneself.

Semen:

Male fluid ejaculations consisting of fluid from the seminal vesicle, prostate gland and sperm. Sperm constitute only about 1 per cent of the total.

The male reproductive fluid that normally contains spermatozoa, the male reproduction germ cell.

Semiautomatic:

A type of firearm firing operation commonly found at criminal events. Operating on the blow-back principle, the trigger must be pulled for each discharge rather than once for a continuous firing as found in fully automatic weapons.

Semi-automatic:

Relating to a gum that uses the force of recoil and mechanical spring action or gas pressure to drive out the empty cartridge after a shot has been fired and to moved another cartridge from the magazine into place for firing; it still requires release of and pressure on the trigger for further shots.

Semi-synthetic narcotics:

The drugs heroin, hydromorphone, oxycodone, etorphine, and diprenorphine,

Semitic writing:

Style of writing from the right- hand side to the left, as is commonly done in Hebrew and Arabic alphabets.

Sentence:

The penality handed down to a defendant by the courts in consideration of crime the party committed.

Serial crimes:

Serious crimes which are characterized by numerous offenses committed by the same suspect or suspects over long periods of time.

Shag:

Slang expression for sexual intercourse. The word is sometimes found offensive by feminists who believe it implies an act of violence towards a passive woman.

Shot hole:

A hole drilled in which dynamite is placed to explode.

Shot in the arm:

Any action designed to build morale.

Shot pattern:

The direction of a spray of bullets that have been discharged from a shotgun.

Shotgun:

A smooth-bore gun that fires multiple pellets. It is aimed and fired from the shoulder.

Shunamitism:

Older men sleeping with young girls in the belief that the closeness of young bodies can rejuvenate them.

Simulated death:

A physiological state in which the victim may appear to be diseased; can be induced by drug overdoses, electrical shock, and many other factors.

Sinsemilla:

From the Spanish, meaning without seed. Commonly refers to high potency marijuana grown in the United States.

Slang:

A career of cheating biking and defrauding. The criminal world.

Slugfest:

A fist fight with everyone involved.

Smack:

Heroin.

Smegma:

A cheesy deposit accumulating under the male foreskin.

Smuff dippers:

Prostitutes.

Snatch:

Female pudendum.

Snuff movie:

A pornographic film in which an actual murder is recorded.

Social withdrawal:

The retreat from social and personal contact that is commonly encountered in the early stages of schizophrenia, when autistic preoccupations lead to aloof detachment and an impaired capacity to communicate with others.

Sodomy:

Anal sex on a male.

Soixante-neuf:

Mutual oral sex from the supposed similarity of the bodies to 69.

Solvability factors:

A method of determining if a specific investigation warrants further investigative effort by examining the presence or absence of common indicators of successful case solution.

Spanish fly:

Canthariden. A drug wrongly believed to be an aphrodisiac. It is made from crushed beetles found in southern Europe. It is an irritant and is potentially a lethal poison.

Spectrophotometer:

An instrument that identifies physical evidence by measuring and recording the absorption spectrum.

Sperm:

Male reproductive cell.

Spiral search:

A crime scene searching method in which the searchers move through the scene in an ever expanding fashion from the center to the outer perimeter.

Split beaver:

Vagina, a stripper, a female teaser.

Spouse abuse:

Pertaining to battery committed by one married partner on the other.

Spunk:

Vulgar term for sperm.

Status offense:

A crime or mischievous act that is an offense when committed by a juvenile and which can be prosecuted only in juvenile curt.

Statute book:

The entire body of legislative law pertaining to a particular jurisdiction, whether published as a whole or not.

Statute of limitations:

A legislative enactment stating that once a certain period of time has elapsed following the commission of a crime no one may be prosecuted for that crime, varics for type of crime and jurisdiction.

Statute, criminal:

An act defining what constitutes a crime and the accompanying punishment. The legislature has amendatory power to revise criminal statutes.

Statute, penal:

A state or federal law that spells out a crime and offense and the degree of punishment that goes with it.

Statute:

A law enacted by legislature; crimes and punishments for such law are commonly defined in state statutes.

Statute:

A law enacted by the legislative branch of a government.

Statutory rape:

Sexual relations with a woman under the age of consent with eighteen being the usual age specified. Statutory rape is viewed as a criminal offense regardless of whether the individual gave her consent. The juvenile is viewed as incapable of making a decision of this nature because of her tender age and maturity level.

Illegal sexual intercourse with a female under a specified age, the female's willingness to engage in the act notwithstanding.

Stay of execution:

A court order that temporarily halts the planned execution of a criminal offender, usually pending further appeals.

Steal:

A specific act of theft. Remove someone else's property without the legal right to do so, with the full intention of keeping the goods,

Stereotypy:

Persistent and mechanical repetition of speech or motor activity.

Sting operation:

A police arrest lactic in which officers simulate criminal operations causing suspects to complete a criminal act. Often used to arrest burglars, fences, and narcotics suspects.

Stipulation:

An agreement between the prosecuting attorney and the defense council to allow a questionable item of evidence to be entered without objection.

Stolen Vehicle Retrieval System:

A method of locating stolen motor vehicles through the placement of hidden transmitters within the vehicle.

Strategic intelligence:

Pertaining to information gathering that provides for long-range planning and decision making.

Stress:

The term is used interchangeably to describe various aversive stimuli of excessive intensity, the physiological, behavioural and subjective responses to them; the context mediating the encounter between the individual and the stressful stimuli; or all of the above as a system.

Strip search:

A crime scene searching method in which the searcher starts at one end of the scene and walks directly across until the opposite end is reached. The searcher then turns and walks back toward the original end searching to the right or left of the original path.

Stupor:

A state characterized by mutism, an absence or profound diminution or blocking of voluntary movement and psychomotor unresponsiveness.

Subpoena:

A writ commanding the person designated to attend a judicial proceeding.

Suffocation:

Death, resulting from an obstruction of air passages to the lungs. It constitutes murder when the nose or mouth are forcibly covered by another person.

Suggestibility:

A type of susceptibility to uncritical acceptance of ideas, beliefs and patterns of behaviour. Suggestibility can be heightened by environmental conditions, drugs and hypnosis.

Suicide pact:

A mutual agreement between two or more people to end their lives in a prearranged manner. The suicide can be simultaneous or one party may kill the other first.

Suicide wounds:

A self-inflicted injury that causes death. A coroner may detect hesitation marks, but death is generally caused by one fatal wound.,

Suicide:

The taking of one's own life. In England, suicide was a common law crime, and at on time was punishable by burial under a pubic highway with a wooden stake driven through the heart. The victim's worldly goods were forfeited to the crown. Today in The US. the forfeiture of property or similar penalties no longer exist. However, attempted suicide is considered a crime in some but, not all, jurisdictions. Rarely does an unsuccessful suicide attempt result in the imposition of a penalty just as long as it did not involve others. A person who causes someone else to take his life as a result of a physical or mental act may face charges of murder or manslaughter.

Suicidology:

The scientific study of suicide, its cause and effects, and methods of prevention.

Summation:

The summing up of a legal proceeding before a jury in which opposing counsel or the judge provides a recapitulation evidence brought forth in the trial so that jurors have a clear understanding before making their decision.

Summons:

A warning or citation to appear in court.

A written order issued by court commanding a defendant to appear at a pacified time to answer criminal charges or supply answers to specific questions from the bench.

Supervision:

The act of confining or watching over another.

Surveillance:

The secretive watching of persons, places, or objects.

Syphilis:

A serious venereal disease which can be fatal in its final or third stage. In man it is more commonly spread homosexually.

T

Tabetic dementia:
Insanity.

Tablet:
A compact pellet of medicine.

Tactical grenade:
A tear gas grenade used for riot control.

Tactical intelligence:
Pertaining to information gathering that is designed to meet short-term planning needs or deal with immediate problems.

Tactical vandalism:
Damage to property committed for some purpose other than monetary gain or acquisition of property.

Tactical vest:
A bulletproof vest.

Take a blow :
To inhale cocaine.

Taking:
The act of having sexual relations with a female under the age of eighteen.

Talwin:
A trade name for the painkiller pentazocone.

Tamper:
The meddle or interfere with something, and by so doing to alter that things, esp. in a corrupt, perverted, or illegal way, e.g., tampering with criminal evidence or a jury. To engage in deceitful negotiations, e.g, accepting a bride.

Tangentiality:

Replying to questions in an oblique and irrelevant way. The central idea is not conveyed.

Tangible evidence:

Evidence that can be seen or touched, in contrast to evidence that comes completely from testimony, e. g., a knife in a homicide trial

Tart:

Is not always an insult as the word has two meanings: Rhyming slang for "sweetheart"- a term of endearment; A prostitute or a woman of cheap and easy virtue, or one who dressed like such a woman.

Tension:

Anxiety with marked motor expression. Patient is conscious of increased muscle tone.

Terrorist International :

A movement that coordinates the action, funding, and the spread of technology among terrorist groups.

Terrorist:

One who uses specific acts of violence, e.g. a bombing, to intimidate or cause apprehension or fear within a civilian population, usually with the aim of attaining some political objective, one who sues or induces terror,

Terrorize:

To fill with horror, terror, or anxiety; to attempt to coerce by threats or acts of violence.

Test case:

A representative trail of which the outcome will likely set legal precedent.

Testimony:

A solemn declaration or affirmation usually made orally by a witness under oath in response to interrogation by an authorized public official.

Tests of suitability:

Three evidence admissibility standards used to determine if an item of evidence will be allowed to have a bearing on a case; evidence must be competent, relevant, and material.

Tetrahydrocannabinol (THC):

The active ingredient in marijuna.

Thanatomania:

An excessive craving to kill oneself or other, from the Greek word for death, "thanatos".

Thanatophile:

One who ,loves death on subjects relating to death such as murder, police work, or murder mysteries.

Thanatophobe:

One who has a fear of death.

Thanatophobia:

The abnormal fear of death.

THC (Tetrahydrocannabinol):

The active ingredient in marijuana.

Theory of transfer:

When two objects come in contact with each other, evidence will be exchanged from one surface to another with traces left at the scene and taken from the scene.

Therapeutic effect:

The drugs or treatment needed to restore one's health.

Thief-taking:

An early method of criminal investigation and apprehension that was based on the premise that only a criminal could successfully apprehend another criminal.

Thought broadcasting:

Patient thinks that others become aware of what he is thinking and thus everyone else is participating in his thought process.

Thought insertion:

A thought appears which is not experienced as belonging to the patient, but as inserted into his mind.

Thought withdrawal:

Patient experiences his thoughts being taken away from him.

Three-legged beaver:

Homosexual

Thrill killing:

Murder committed simply for the excitement or pleasure it elicits.

Throttle:

To straggle or choke.

Throttlehold:

A brutal or savage strangling grasp

Throttling:

Strangulation.

Throwaway:

A juvenile delinquent who is out of the control of his parents.

Time bomb:

An explosive device designed to detonate at a predetermined time

Time served:

The total of all the time spent in legal confinement, including the time served before conviction and sentencing.

Tochus:

(Tochus, Tokus)- U.S = backside, buttocks, anus from Yiddish tokhesi: Hebrew tohat- beneath.

Tolerance:

Decrease in response to a drug that occurs with continued

use of the drug.

Toolmark:

An impression resulting from forceful contact between a tool and the surface area of an object.

Toss-off:

To masturbate.

Toss-pot:

Although an insult, this expression is not obscene. It means a heavy drinker or a drunkard.

Toughie:

A hoodlum; a tough guy.

Trajectory:

The flight path of a projectile, such as a bullet discharged from a firearm.

Transvestite:

A persona who derives pleasure from wearing cloths of the opposite sex. Almost al transvestites are heterosexual men although some homosexuals do cross dress.

Trespass ab initio (lat):

A phrase used to describe a lawful or innocent entry which becomes a trespass from the beginning because the conduct after the lawful entry constitutes trespass by an abuse of privilege.

Trespass:

The entry into or upon another's property without permission or lawful authority, or any illegal interference with a person's property or rights.

Trespasser:

One who commits the crime of trespass.

Trial court:

The first court to litigate a matter, the court of original jurisdiction, as opposed to an appellate court.

Trial:

A formal judicial examination to determine if the defendant is guilty of the crime as charged. It is the part of a judicial proceeding that comes after preliminary hearings and pleadings, which includes testimony and evidence, opening and closing arguments, and the verdict.

Triangulation:

A crime scene measuring method in which measurements are taken from two fixed points to the evidence object, thus forming a triangle as a frame of reference.

Tribaclism:

Sexual activity between two women involving rubbing the genitals together.

Trick:

Intercourse provided by a prostitute.

Trickery:

The art of deception.

Truck hijacking:

A form of vehicle robbery in which trucks are seized for the valuable cargo contained within.

Tush:

U.S. slang. The buttocks.

Twat (less commonly, Twot)- U.K:

Vagina, also a term of common abuse. U.S: sometimes means buttocks.

U

Ultraviolet light:
Radiation situated beyond the violet, visible end of the light spectrum.

Uncock:
To take a gun's hammer out of a cocked position.

Unconscious person:
A dead body, as described by a police radio dispatcher.

Unconscious:
Being unaware of one's own actions, e.g., due to sleepwalking.

Uncover:
To disclose or bring to light.

Undercover agent:
A law enforcement officer who infiltrates criminal gangs or operations without revealing his true purpose. He collects evidence which is later used in a criminal trial.

Undercover operations:
Pertaining to the fictitious identities assumed by police officers and the roles they play to accomplish an investigative objective.

Underground:
A secret organization of citizens, especially in an occupied region, fighting for freedom until liberation is achieved. Anything done in secret

Unearth:
To discover or make known.

Unfetter:

To remove confining fetters.

Uniform crime:

Annual statistical reports, published by the FBI, that analyze and record crime rates in the United States.

Uniforms:

Police officers who are assigned to a patrol and wear regulation uniforms.

Unlawful act:

A deed which is prohibited or unauthorized by law.

Contrary to, prohibited or unauthorized by law.

Unlawful assembly:

In common law, a planned meeting between specified number of persons who intend to disturb the peace with a forceful demonstration. It is considered a rout if they initiate steps toward disrupting the peace. It is a riot if the plan is actually carried out.

Unlawful entry:

Entry upon property through fraudulent or unlawful means, but without using force i.e., upon property through fraudulent or unlawful means, but without using force.

Unlawful picketing:

Picket in which is dishonest or involves misrepresentations or lies.

Unlawful:

By breaking the law; wrongfully.

Unreasonable search and seizure :

Any search or seizure made without a warrant or legal excuse or one executed with a warrant by lacking probable cause.

Unwritten law:

That body of the law which, while not reflected in statutes in nevertheless observed and administered in court, e.g., judicial precedents.

Utmost resistance:

Refers to the principle recognized in some jurisdictions that for a rape charge to be sustained, the victim must have offered utmost resistance.

V

Vacate:

To make or render a legal decision or a record void.

Vagrancy:

In common law, the condition of being transient, without visible means of support, without lawful purpose or object, and refusing to work, although physically capable. Vagrancy is defined differently by different states. Many vagrancy statutes have been found unconstitutional for various reasons, e.g., they are too vague, punish behavior which is not criminal, infringe upon personal liberty, and violate due process.

Vagrant act:

An English law punishing idle disorderly persons. Subsequent revision to the statute have distinguished vagrants from petty street criminals.

Vagrant:

One who is transient without visible means of support and refuses to seek or accept work, although the support of others, either though begging or petty thievery.

Vagrom:

A vagrant.

Valentino:

A thief who victimizes women. It refers to the 1920s cinematic idol Rudolph Valentino.

Valium:

A trade name for the central nervous system depressant Diazepam.

Vampire:

One who is believed to rise from the dead at night and search for and suck the blood of living persons.

Vandal:

A person, usually a juvenile delinquent, who deliberately or recklessly destroys or defaces property belonging to others.

Vandalism:

The deliberate destruction of property, i.e. literary and artistic works.

Vehicle identification number:

The metal plate now referred to as the permanent identification number. Data on the plate include vehicle make, model, year of manufacture, plant location, engine type and sequential production number.

Vehicular homicide:

A murder caused by the careless operation of a motor vehicle. Statutes vary concerning the elements of the crime but may encompass both negligence and intentional behavior.

Vehicular manslaughter:

Bringing about the death of another through the reckless operation of a motor vehicle.

Vehicular weapon:

Any car, truck motorcycle or automotive vehicle used as an assault weapon by its driver.

Vendetta:

The sworn act of revenge against a person or family who has gravely offended another party.

Venereal:

Pertaining to sex, especially transmittal of disease through intercourse.

Venireman:

A prospective or current member of a jury.

Venue:

The proper locality in which a court having jurisdiction may hear and decide a case. A judge may order a change of venue if the believes that a community's citizens are predisposed to reach a certain verdict, e.g., when there has been substantial pre-trial publicity of the crime,

Venus' curse:

Any form venereal disease.

Verbal:

An oral confession disease.

Verbatim:

Notes or a formal statement taken in the same words actually used; word for word.

Verdict:

Derived from verdicts, meaning a true declaration. It is the official decision made by a jury or judge concerning the defendant's guilt or innocence. In criminal cases, the verdict, which must be unanimous, is typically announced to the judge in an open court.

Vibrator:

A dildo with an electric motor causing it to vibrate. Usually, but not always driven by batteries. Can be used-to massage various body areas particularly the genitals.

Vice ladies:

Female criminals involved in extortion, mugging, prostitution, drug trafficking, and gambling.

Vice:

Moral corruption, especially crimes involving immorality; prostitution, pederasty, illegal gambling, found, etc,

Victim compensation:

Financial or other forms of assistance given to crime victims by the state, especially those victimized in person-to-person crimes.

Victim precipitated crime:

Criminal offenses which involve a conscious or unconscious action by the victim which is a causative factor in their victimization.

Victim:

A person who has suffered direct harm from a criminal offender during the execution of a crime, e.g., murder or robbery.

Victimal:

Involving or being, a victim, the opposite of criminal.

Victimity:

Pertaining or being a victim as opposed to criminality

Victimization:

To condition of being a victim.

Victimize:

To defraud or cheat someone.

Victimol:

The study of the relationship between criminals and victims. One who conducts research into the field. That which relates to such a study.

Victimological:

Relating to study of the criminal victim relationship.

A professional who conducts research on the criminal-victim relationship a scholar in this particular endeavor.

The study of the relationship between criminals and victims, and the impact of crime on a society. It is the opposite of criminology .

Victimous:

Relating to or being a victim,

Videotaping:

A visual and aural method of recording suspect confessions, admissions, or statements given by victims or witnesses. Also used to record crime scenes, undercover operations, and other investigative operations.

Vigilante:

A member of an outlaw gang or band of angry citizens that has decided to take maters into its own hands and punish an offender without the proper legal sanctions. From the Spanish word, vigilante, meaning a guard or watchman.

Vigilantism:

A war against crime by a self-appointed citizen's law enforcement groups that, ironically, breaks the law to enforce it.

Vindicate:

To find one not guilty or free of blame.

Vindictive vandalism:

Defacing, stealing, or destroying the property of another for revenge.

Violation:

Any action that breaches a laws, official rule, or obligation. Penal statutes frequently classify a violation as the ravishment or sexual abuse of another person. The crime of breaking a prison parole.

Violence:

Physical force which injures, abuses, or damage, The unauthorized or unfounded use of force, frequently accompanied by fury, outrage, or strong emotion.

Violent Criminal Apprehension Program (of FBI):

A data collection program in which specific violent crimes are reported to the FBI and studied for similarities in method of operation. The crimes of murder, rape, arson, and child sexual abuse are particularly well suited for serial analyses.

Violent death:

A sudden dearth caused by the violent actions of another, distinguish from a natural death which is the deterioration of the vital organs due to disease or old age.

Violent offense:

Crimes involving the extreme use of physical force, e.g., murder.

Violent:

That which is characterized by physical force, esp. extreme, sudden, unfounded unauthorized, or furious force.

Voice stress evaluator:

A device that monitors the vocal quality of an individual producing a graph-like reading indicating the possibility of deception.

Voiceprint:

A method of speaker identification in which the pitch, rate of speech, and articulation are evaluated, as well as certain anatomical factors not under the speaker's conscious control; also known as sound spectrograph.

An oral representation of person's voice created through spectrography. It is used primarily in criminal identification

Voluntary confession:

An admission of guilt made by an individual who has not been coerced or otherwise improperly induced into an act of self-incrimination.

Voluntary informant:

Any individual who provides information to the police without ulterior motive or payment.

Voluntary:

A statement given freely by a criminal to a police officer.

Voodoo:

A ritualistic religion derived from African ancestor worship involving trance like communications and propitiatory rites with animalistic deities.

Voodooism:

The art or practice of voodoo or witchcraft.

Vouch:

To give corroborating evidence or verification.

Voyeur:

One who is sexually satisfied from observing but not joining a sex act, or from watching someone else undress, esp. if the voyeur is seen by the person or persons he is watching.

Voyeurism or Peeping Tomism:

Pleasure derived from watching other people undress or having sex. Usually done in secret. It is rare, but possible for them to go further and harm the victim.

A deviation in which a person derives his pleasure from viewing but not participating in sexual acts. The act of watching a person undress, or in a state of complete nudity. The presence of the voyeur or peeping tom need not be known to the victim, but usually the humiliation caused by the victim's realization that be or she is observed increases the sexual satisfaction for the voyeur. Surreptitious observation of another for sexual gratification.

Vulnerability analysis:

A security evaluation of a structure by trained crime prevention officers to determine points of risk regarding crime victimization.

W

Wanger:

An informal agreement or contract between two or more individuals who have mutually agreed to transfer ownership of property or surrender a specified amount of money to either party depending on the uncertain outcome of a particular event or the determination of disputed fact; a gamble a bet.

Waive:

To relinquish one's rights.

Waiver:

The international and voluntary relinquishment of a known right, privilege, or claim The abandonment or disposal of stolen property during escape from the scene of the crime.

Walkie-talkie:

Portable two –way communication device

Wank:

Masturbation

Wanker:

Insult, one given self-abuse.

Warrant:

A court-issued document that allows a law enforcement officer of make an arrest, search specified premises, or take other actions specified in the warrant, e,.g. seizure of property.

Welsh-style:

Anal intercourse.

West case:

A case in which two inmates so closely resembled each other in physical characteristics that the traditional Bertillon method of identification was discredited.

Whist:

A card game with a number of variations played throughout the world. Cards are dealt one at a time, usually to four persons playing in teams of two. One point is awarded for each trick obtained after the sixth trick. The winning team earns points by subtracting the number of points scored by the losing team from Seven. A total of seven points is needed to win the game.

White-collar crime:

Pertaining to business, professional, and consumer frauds, or to various other criminal offenses that occur to customers or clients.

Whore:

A female who engages in sexual intercourse for payment or to fulfill obsessive desire for sex.

Whoredom:

Prostitution

Whorehouse:

A house of prostitution.

Whoremonger:

A pimp.

Whoreson:

The illegitimate male offspring of a whore.

Whorish:

Characteristic of prostitute

Whorl fingerprint:

Fingerprint patterns which encircle a central pattern classified as plain, central pocket loop, double loop, or accidental whorls.

Whorl:

A type of finger print.

Witch:

A female believed to have supernatural powers, usually for evil purposes and usually in collusion with a devil or demon.

Withdraw symptoms:

Physical and / or mental effects produced by sudden or gradual withdrawl of drug usage. Symptoms may include anxiety, muscle cramping, vomiting, and general nausea.

Withdrawal state:

A group of symptoms of variable clustering and degree of severity occurring on absolute or relative withdrawal of a substance after persistent use of that substance.

Withdrawal:

A physical and emotional state common with individual addicted to narcotics. The absence of the drug causes abnormal bodily functions as the physical need for the narcotic increase with its deprivation.

Withholding of evidence:

To suppress or destroy evidence with the knowledge that the evidence is wanted in a court proceeding, or sought by law enforcement officials. May constitute an obstruction of justice.

Without her consent:

A term used in many statutes regarding rape. The term means that sexual penetration during rape occurred against the will of the victim, and that the victim resisted the attack.

Witness box:

An enclosed area from where a witness gives testimony from during a courtroom trial.

Witness stand:

The location in a courtroom from where witness or defendants give testimony during a trial.

Witness, material :

A witness who, during a criminal trial, provides extremely

important testimony that is integral to either the case for the defense or for the prosecution. Often the material witness is required to post bond for his appearance or is protected or confined by law enforcement agencies until such a time that he is able to testify.

Witness, adverse:

A witness who gives evidence prejudicial to the examining party; one whose relationship to the examining party indicates that his testimony may be prejudiced against that party.

Witness:

An observer who sees or knows by personal presence and perception and/or a person who is requested to testify in a case or before a judicial proceeding.

Writ of habeas corpus:

A legal document calling for immediate judicial review of the circumstances pertaining to the continued confinement of an accused individual; designed to obtain the prompt release of a person who is unlawfully detained.

Writ of quo warranto:

A civil court writ sometimes used in criminal proceedings to challenge authority which is being unlawfully asserted.

Wrong, public:

Injury to a community by actions taken in violation of public rights.

Wrongdoer:

A person who breaks laws, either ethical or judicial.

Wrongdoing:

Breaking laws or committing evil deeds.

X

X-rated:

Movies for adult only, usually. Pornographic films depicting sexuality and especially sex deviation. May also be rated as XX or XXX. An area where houses of prostitution, shops selling pornographic items, and gambling dens operate.

Xylocaine:

A lindocane trade name, used by doctors and dentists as a local anesthetic.

XYY syndrome:

A genetic defect in certain human males wherein they possess an extra Y chromosome. Males with this syndrome are often overly aggressive.

Z

Zones:
Three division that make up the writing space.

Zoophilia:
Bestiality.